A CONCISE HISTORY OF FLY FISHING

GLENN LAW

THE LYONS PRESS
Guilford, Connecticut
An imprint of The Globe Pequot Press

The Lyons Press is an imprint of The Globe Pequot Press.

FRONTISPIECE: *Yellow Fly and Ruddy Fly,* two of Dame Juliana Berners' patterns.

All color photography by Egmont Van Dyck.

Illustrated by Rod Walinchus, Livingston, Montana.

10 9 8 7 6 5 4 3 2 1

Printed in the United States of America

ISBN 1-59228-061-7

Library of Congress Cataloging-in-Publication Data is available on file.

4

CONTENTS

There is, indeed, this excuse for the novice, that, going back to the authorities of the past after much experiment, he will find that they know in substance all, or practically all, that, apart from the advance of mechanical conveniences and entomological science, is known in the present day.

— G.E.M. Skues
   Minor Tactics of the Chalk Stream, 1910

The history of fly fishing has always fascinated me. I suppose if you enjoy the sport as I do, knowing where it began, who contributed to it, and the milestones along the way all make it so interesting.

I have read several books on the history of the sport but none that I thought were historically accurate, until now. I can only assume that the authors of several books did a good job concerning the older facets of the sport. But when they wrote about some of the anglers I had been around, I found many things credited to these people that were simply not true. Either the author was acquainted with the angler being written about, or the angler was great at developing publicity kind to him. As a result, the author gave the angler credit for developments or accomplishments that were not truly his.

So I was a bit apprehensive about offering a history of the sport. Any apprehension disappeared, however, when I learned that Glenn Law had been chosen to write the book. And when I received the manuscript, I found it was by far the best history of fly fishing I'd ever read. Glenn has not fallen in the trap other writers have. This book, at least in the areas where I have had experience, is accurate. Not only that, but through his fresh and creative approach, Glenn has made a real contribution to the way we enjoy the sport.

Glenn, a lifelong fly fisherman, is the editor of *Florida Sportsman Magazine,* a publication he has been with for six years. For the past 10, he's fished saltwater exclusively, and the 10 years before that was a licensed outfitter in Montana, guiding, fishing, and teaching casting. He's a critically acclaimed essayist and has published in most of the major outdoor magazines. Needless to say, he's an excellent writer. You're going to enjoy this history of our sport.

Bernard "Lefty" Kreh
Hunt Valley, Maryland

INTRODUCTION

I'm not an historian, I'm a fisherman, and as such I'm intensely interested in all things that have to do with fly fishing.

So why a history of fly fishing? After all, what do history and reading have to do with catching fish?

With fly fishing, they have everything to do with it. At least they do if you ever want to do more than hire a guide who will choose your fly, tie it on for you, and then tell you exactly where to cast.

The challenge of analysis and imitation that defines the sport places a premium on information, and for this reason, the history, like the history of any subject, can save us a lot of time. It's also a pleasurable facet of fly fishing to tie the discoveries of the past to the practice of the present. It roots us in the sport, if we need any additional passion for it.

In the learning and practice of a sport as consuming as fishing with a fly, there are touchstones along the way, points of reference, or passages, if you will. My memories of learning to fish are not yours. There are people, places, and books that remain significant along my angling road: Gayle Back, Jack Sebzda, Rock Creek, Joe Brooks, the Malleo, Bearmouth. Some of these are mine, an integral part of my own fishing history and life. Some others share. There are a substantial number of these touchstones common to all of us — this is the tradition and history of fly fishing.

The point at which we encounter significant ideas determines a lot about the kind of angler we inevitably become, how we go about our business on the stream. And because fly fishing has a way of infiltrating our very being, I suppose our fishing experience reverberates in the people we are day to day, as well. As in nearly all endeavors, the more we know, the more we understand, and the more we enjoy ourselves on the water.

Why this, a concise history?

For one thing, it's never been done quite like this before. More specialized, more academic, and lengthier studies have been done, as have plenty of shorter ones, mostly as introductory chapters to books. There has been a need, then, for a collection of common touchstones, high points, and significant incidents in the history of fly fishing that contribute to a general literacy in the origins of our sport.

I hope this concise history provides you that at least — a general literacy in the sport.

When someone refers to the "cunning brown wink," you'll know whence it came and the cultural warfare that accompanied it. Witness two anglers discussing the relative merits of a Royal Wulff versus a Gordon Quill and you'll know the argument didn't begin this season.

A history such as this presents its own problems. Because angling is an individual pursuit rather than a team or spectator sport, most of it takes place where no one is watching, without record or evidence it ever happened. The only history we are able to piece together comes down through the writing of those who not only fished but also wrote.

What then of the anglers who have been interested in catching fish and didn't have the wherewithal to publish, nor the interest in announcing their methods?

I'm reminded of an observation made by Russell Chatham regarding expert fly casters and the essential privacy of the sport. "Put a few hundred grand on the line and no doubt some very cool hands would begin appearing at casting tournaments," he says in *The Angler's Coast*.

The anglers themselves are the real history and the part we'll never know. That's also the part we re-create every time we go astream.

This history, then, must concern itself with people, and specifically people who wrote about their fishing.

It's often difficult to separate the fishing history from the literature from the personalities. Where possible we'll try to keep an ear tuned for the fishing, but at times it may seem we've wandered far. Because fly fishing isn't a spectator sport, fishermen and writers both appear as sum and substance of the history.

Necessarily, personalities are a big part of the sport. This is fine, and though it may seem like so much name-dropping, it really is more than that. Can you talk about the history of football and not mention Rockne? Can you discuss jazz and ignore Coltrane?

The names are as much a part of fishing as great ball handlers or improvisational geniuses are to those disciplines.

Get used to it. It's OK. There has never been an important development in fly fishing that didn't appear first on the water, then later in the words of a writer.

At the same time, any attempt to record fishing history becomes a partial history of fishing literature. That, too, is inescapable to a certain extent.

It's easy to err too far in this direction, though. In order to avoid producing a history of angling literature, I've stuck to the seminal works for each of the major developmental periods. At times the history of the literature and the history of the fishing are inexorably linked. At times it's easy to wander off in the literature itself. I've tried to avoid this. If the literature intrigues you, have at it. There are enough references in the bibliography to get you started.

Trout fishing occupies the greatest part of this history. There's a good reason for this. It's the backbone of the sport.

Fly fishing began on trout streams. The tackle, technique, and theory developed in the pursuit of trout. While it is possible to spend an angling career fly fishing and never fish for trout, who would want to? Fly fishermen born and raised on saltwater are still fly fishermen, but lacking knowledge of their sources, the traditions of trout fishing, they are missing a big part of the sport. They may argue this point. If they do, they are wrong.

This is not a history of specialization, and as such, trout fishing is the heart of the game.

What I have accumulated here is conventional knowledge, the common touchstones of the sport, the things we all need to know about. If there's a significant person in fly-fishing history, a familiar quotation, a widely acknowledged turning point in fly fishing, I hope I've not overlooked it.

If it's scholarship you are after, there are plenty of other places to find it. If it's basic literacy in the background of the sport, I've tried to provide everything you'll need. It's a dilettante's view of 4,000 years of fly fishing.

In conversations struck up in bars and tackle shops; in your streamside musings; staring out the window over the top of your desk; when you wake up in the middle of the night and fishing is on your mind; or when you look back down the road you traveled to become the fisherman you are, I hope this history is useful.

Glenn Law
South Miami, 1994

OVERLEAF: *Fan-Wing Royal Coachman, created by Theodore Gordon, American fly fisherman, writer, and tyer.*

CHAPTER ONE

ANCIENT WRITING ON THE WALL TO THE BEGINNINGS OF A LITERATE TRADITION

The history of fly fishing lies somewhere buried with the beginnings of angling itself. In the dim and distant fogs of antiquity it lies, when some hairy hominid felt a stirring of pleasure in acquiring sustenance from a lake or stream or river. It becomes impossible to separate subsistence and survival from sport.

Chances are there has always been an element of sport in fishing. Even those who fished to survive or to provide for the tribe surely must have enjoyed what they were doing. The mystery of life beneath the surface of the water, an element that excludes us, compels our curiosity, our intellect, and our imagination so universally and so completely that we can state it is so, and has always been so, without fear of contradiction. And it runs that strong still. Our very identity as anglers is clear proof.

It's hard to imagine that in the course of gathering fish for survival the challenge to do a little better next time wasn't a constant. A successful fishing trip led one to look for equal success the next time, and a bad day of fishing, as we well know, can only get better. This is what keeps us going back again and again, and it only stands to reason that this has been so for as long as we've sought to pull fish out of the water.

Likely the first inkling of sport entered the picture when the first one got away. Fishing is, after all, a constant exercise in optimism, looking forward to the next time, dreaming it will be just a little better.

The only evidence we have of the fishing that went on is the hard goods that remain. We're pretty much stuck with reconstructing a lot of information through artifacts. In this case, artifacts means hooks.

Evidence of early man's infatuation with what would become our sport is fragmented. The forerunner of the fish hook, the gorge, can be traced accurately to archeological diggings in France. Designed to be buried in a bait, then swallowed by the fish to catch sideways in its throat, the gorge was a moderately efficient tool. It could be fashioned from a variety of materials at hand, and when it worked, it worked well. It was not well suited to catch-and-release fishing, but at the time it enjoyed the greatest popularity, this was not a concern.

Other varieties of hooks fashioned from bone, wood, and pointy animal parts, like insect legs and bird claws, all did their jobs as intended.

For hooks to really begin to offer any hint of providing an armature around which an insect imitation could be fashioned, they must first be made of metal. Basic metallurgy was requisite for the development of even the most rudimentary artificial fly.

Fish hooks that fit this criterion have been unearthed in the ancient city of Ur on the Euphrates from around 2600 B.C.[1] Hooks at this time were made of copper.

More to our interest, a wall painting in an Egyptian tomb dating circa 1400 B.C. shows a seated angler holding a rod to which are attached several strands of line. Over a curiously square-cornered stream full of fish, most remarkable of all is the unmistakable stonefly fluttering toward the ceiling.[2]

Oriental origins of angling are not quite as fragmented, but we still must be content with bits and pieces of reference and illustration to piece together any history, and even with that, there is never a lot of continuity.

Fishing in general was well known and recognized as a contemplative pastime in ancient China. This isn't surprising considering China had the technology required to produce tackle adequate to provide enjoyable angling. China had the raw materials in abundance — bamboo for rods, silk for lines, and a tradition of metallurgy that flourished in the Shang dynasty (1766-1122 B.C.).

Chiang Tzu-Ya, late in the Zhou dynasty (1122-221 B.C.), presented a splendid case for the moral and contemplative aspects of fishing, and himself went so far as to fish without a hook in the bait. This was clearly a dead end technically, but as a forerunner of modern catch-and-release practice it must be so noted.

Not to be outdone in the esoteric, Chang Chi-Ho fished in the eighth century, Ernest Schwiebert records in *Trout,* without hook or bait, in order to muse undisturbed.

Schwiebert also stretches our imagination a bit, speculating that golden hooks may have been adorned with kingfisher feathers in use during the Zhou dynasty. He acknowledges the feathers could have been attached to the line, some sort of good-luck charm, but he clearly wants to insinuate some sort of streamer fly had been devised. This bit of speculation would have pushed the appearance of the artificial fly back about 400 years before it was generally acknowledged to have appeared, when Aelian described the first fly dressing.

Schwiebert also reports the development of the fishing reel, tracing it to China 1,500 years ago, a good long time before the generally accepted European appearance of the reel in the mid 1600s. Paintings reproduced in *The History of Chinese Science* by Joseph Needham clearly show fishermen with reels. This is something not entirely outlandish given China's developed weaving industry, which would have made the bobbin and the spindle common appliances not unsuited to angling applications.[3]

Within our own occidental tradition, the first mention of a fly in literature has been commonly accepted to be Aelian. In *Fishing From the Earliest Times,* William Radcliffe raises the possibility that the earliest reference to the artificial fly appears in the writings of Martial, a Roman poet, a couple hundred years before Aelian, with these lines:

Who has not seen the scarus rise,
Decoyed, and killed by fraudful flies?

Radcliffe entertains a bit of a quandary here, with a discussion of the translation of these lines. The key word is "flies," which can be translated either *musco,* meaning moss, or *musca,* meaning fly. What follows is a lengthy discussion of the proper translation of the original Latin. The mention, however, is brief, and even if the word was "fly," this would push the first mention back only a couple of hundred years.

Because Radcliffe is above all else an impeccable scholar, these things take on a great significance and take up a great deal of speculative space in his book. Having examined all sides of the issue, the common species that could be deceived by moss and those that could be deceived by an artificial fly, he concludes this is the first mention of the artificial fly in fishing and further concludes it is a method which has been in existence for quite some time.

This is a historical phenomenon that will recur throughout our journey through the history of fly fishing. Time and time again, a technique, an idea, an article of tackle will appear in the literature, and closer investigation will reveal it has been around a while. It's not at all unusual for an angling practice to be pretty well entrenched and widespread before anyone ever writes about it. It's one of the problems in separating the fishing history from the literary history of fishing.

Certainly the most widely accepted earliest reference to fly fishing appeared in *De Animalium Natura* by Aelian 2,000 years ago, with the often-quoted business about "a river called the Astraeus, and in this river are fish with spotted skins."

Because it's such a grand starting point for our traditions, here's the full translation of the section dealing with fly fishing for trout. This particular translation is that of O. Lambert from *Angling Literature in England* as quoted by Radcliffe in *Fishing From the Earliest Times:*

> *I have heard of a Macedonian way of catching fish, and it is this: between Beroea and Thessalonica runs a river called the Astraeus, and in it there are fish with speckled skins; what the natives of the country call them you had better ask the Macedonians. These fish feed on a fly peculiar to the country, which hovers on the river. It is not like flies found elsewhere, nor does it resemble a wasp in appearance, nor in shape would one justly describe it as a midge or a bee, yet it has something of each of these. In boldness it is like a fly, in size you might call it a midge, it imitates the colour of a wasp, and it hums like a bee. The natives generally call it the* Hippouros.*
>
> *These flies seek their food over the river, but do not escape the observation of the fish swimming below. When then the fish observes a fly on the surface, it swims quietly up, afraid to stir the water above, lest it should scare away its prey; then coming up by its shadow, it opens its mouth gently and gulps down the fly, like a wolf carrying off a sheep from the fold or an eagle a goose from the farmyard; having done this it goes beneath the rippling water.*

Now though the fisherman know of this, they do not use these flies at all for bait for fish; for if a man's hand touch them, they lose their natural colour, their wings wither, and they become unfit food for the fish. For this reason they have nothing to do with them, hating them for their bad character; but they have planned a snare for the fish, and get the better of them by their fisherman's craft.

They fasten red (crimson red) wool round a hook, and fix on to the wool two feathers which grow under a cock's wattles, and which in colour are like wax. Their rod is six feet long, and their line is the same length. Then they throw their snare, and the fish, attracted and maddened by the colour, comes straight at it, thinking from the pretty sight to get a dainty mouthful; when, however, it opens its jaws, it is caught by the hook and enjoys a bitter repast, a captive.[4]

Aelian has herein described the essential problem in fly fishing: how to catch fish that are feeding on flies over the river when those flies cannot be fastened to a hook in order to catch the fish.

John Waller Hills, in his *History of Fly Fishing for Trout*, dismisses this mention as an isolated incident with no inherent value of its own, without merit until a modern writer quoted it as a curiosity. He elects a tip of the hat, then moves on, which is about all we can do. However, it is significant that this description by Aelian, while lacking substantial contribution to the traditions of angling as they will come down to us, serves to present the fundamental problem in fly fishing: the intentional imitation of a specific insect on which a fish is feeding. Curiosity is the stuff of historians, and it doesn't pay to pass observations over cynically.

This is the fundamental problem addressed every time the angler goes astream, and it is significant that Aelian stated it when he did. While neither his fly dressing, his purposes and intent, his tackle, nor his techniques are recognizable as the backbone of our angling traditions, it must be handed him, he identified the problem: catching a fish that is feeding on something too delicate to skewer on a hook for bait.

It would still be a couple of thousand years before we acquired a written attempt to codify the solutions to that fundamental problem, and when that document appeared, it provided the basis for all our fishing.

Let's wander a bit then in the waning years of the Middle Ages, when we find society emerging from several centuries of xenophobic, self-imposed exile.

Travel and communication were on the increase. Modern printing was in its infancy, and for the first time a semblance of mass dissemination of literature and ideas was possible. With this awakening came the first true literature of fly fishing, a genuine record of our sport hand in hand with printing, and ultimately, a description of fly fishing that could well serve as a textbook today.

OVERLEAF: *Four Dame Juliana Berners patterns — Maure Fly, Wasp Fly, Ruddy Fly, and The Black Leaper — and a facsimile of the opening page of* Treatyse of Fysshynge wyth an Angle.

Saloman in hys paraboles se

spirit maket a flo**_ing a_**

feyre age & ionge

so I aske questyon wyche byn

cause to re e a man to a mery sp

to my symp discrescion it semy

honest d **es** and games in wyc

joytl with owt any ans Tha

pat good & honeste portes by c

fare age and longe **Therfor n**

of iiij good disporte **d** honest g

sey of huntyng hackyng fowlyng

namely anglyng with a or a y

a hole per of to tre as my s

suffi th for he seyde reson o

also for the reson of physyke mayd

Si tibi deficiant medici medici

Hec tria mens leta labor & mod

CHAPTER TWO

WRITTEN LEGACY
AND THE INIMITABLE
DAME JULIANA

I always tried to ignore Juliana Berners, prioress of the nunnery of Sopwell who published *The Treatyse of Fysshynge wyth an Angle,* a chapter in *The Boke of Saint Albans,* in 1496, acknowledged as the first English essay on fishing.

From the first time I read about her in Joe Brooks' *Trout Fishing* and every subsequent encounter, and there have been a lot of them, it seems she was mentioned to inject academic credibility more than anything else, to any history of fishing, and fly fishing in particular. She always seemed to me to be a convenient claim to authenticity.

Perhaps she failed to catch my interest because her contributions were never mentioned, just the fact that she produced one of the first angling documents. As well, those were times when I wanted to get on the stream, when what was new and around the corner was what would catch fish. Esoterica held little of my attention, and I had yet to learn that the more you look at what is new, the older it really is.

The very existence of Juliana is a bit of speculation by academics devoted to reconstructing this stretch of history. Her identity and contribution to English literature had been questioned, discussed, refuted, and finally somewhat settled by historians of English long before fly fishermen ever laid claim to her. Placed in a cultural as well as sporting perspective, Berners is fascinating. Under closer examination, Dame Juliana and the *Treatyse* emerge as an engaging piece of history in English culture and in fly fishing, both the literature and the sport.

THE LITERARY TRADITION EMERGES

The entire literature of sport throughout the Middle Ages was written in French. Any examples so far uncovered in English have been translations made after the originals. It is one of these — *The Master of Game,* translated by the Duke of York, Henry IV's master of game — that appears as the first sporting book in English, and in fact becomes the model for what will become a long-running and successful formula for sporting books.

The structure of the sporting book that emerged at this time would provide the framework for every fishing book that followed — even modern fly-fishing books have the same structure more or less intact.

The formula is simple and effective. A prologue provides a description of the sport and often compares it with other, similar sports. In the fifteenth century, hawking, hunting, and angling were commonly contrasted, then the merits of one sport — the one that was the subject of the book — promoted in contrast to the other sports. A modern treatment would find the author singing the praises of fly fishing as a more engaging, more challenging, or more satisfying method of angling than, say, spin fishing. Natural history, techniques, and equipment were then discussed, forming the body of information of the chosen sport. In conclusion an epilogue was offered, sometimes including rules or recommendations for proper conduct or behavior.

This structure is familiar and comfortable to us. We have seen it all our reading and sporting lives. It originated with *The Master of Game.* It is the form that would impress itself on every sporting book since. Not surprisingly, it is the structure adopted by Berners in the first English sporting book, *The Boke of Saint Albans.*

The Boke of Saint Albans was a compilation of essays covering heraldry, hawking, and hunting. It was first printed in English in 1486. Its style and structure unmistakably draw without apology from its predecessors, for this was a time when literary property did not exist. Wenkyn de Worde published the second edition of *The Boke* in 1496 and included a fourth chapter, *Treatyse of Fysshynge wyth an Angle,* hereafter *TFA.* This is the first full-length publication dealing with fly fishing, and the authorship is credited to Dame Juliana Berners.

Let's look first at Juliana and where she fits in, then we'll look at her contribution to fly fishing.

Juliana Berners is today the name inexorably linked with *TFA.* Challenges have been raised on the issue of her authorship, as they have to her very existence over the years. The questions have not been entirely settled, though plenty of serious study has gone into both verifying and negating her contribution. Here is what has been pretty well established about her.

Known variously as a copyist, collector, and perhaps not even a fisher, a noblewoman well versed in the field sports — and located conveniently near the River Ver — Berners was the prioress of the nunnery of Sopwell, northwest of London. Through the fifteenth century her name appears variously as Barnes, Bernes, and Berners. It was not until the second edition of *The Boke of Saint Albans* published in 1496 that her name was even mentioned.

On evidence of the Bernes name, she was entered into the lore of the printed English language, credited with these things: She was the first woman to publish in English. *The Boke of Saint Albans* was the first sporting book published in English, and it appeared only nine years after Caxton printed the first book in English.

By all reports and evidence, *The Boke of Saint Albans* was a bestseller, leading the list that numbered some 800 volumes published by Robert Copland prior to 1530.

All extraneous details and academic endeavors aside, Juliana Berners' name is unquestionably linked with the 1496 edition of *The Boke*, the one that contained *TFA*, and her name shall be linked with it forever — probably even if it is proven at some time that she had nothing to do with it. Such is the nature of legend and historical fact.

As mentioned earlier, Berners was more an article of literary history than angling history for a couple of centuries. It was not until the time of the first Walton revival that Juliana became an issue in the sport. The legend of Berners and the *TFA* enters the annals of angling history in the 1760 edition of *The Compleat Angler,* edited by John Hawkins. This, the eighth edition of Walton, was the standard edition to be reprinted many times through the nineteenth century. When Hawkins picked up the legend of Juliana, it was already well developed. He attributed her established role in angling history to previous scholarship, and that was that.

Berners' importance gained attention in 1559, according to John McDonald in *Quill Gordon,* when historians and chroniclers began to record the end of medieval times as they dissolved into modern time and the Renaissance. By 1619 she had been described as an "illustrious female, eminently endowed with superior qualities both mental and personal" (John Bale, 1559) and "a manlike woman endowed with brilliant gifts of nature." (John Pits, 1619)[5]

So the academic students of the first English writers, the notes, writing, and speculation by various early English collectors and antiquaries, as McDonald calls them, are well documented. McDonald himself made a rather thorough case for the authorship by a bit of investigative scholarship, matching handwritten margin notes with established facts, and pretty much established the authenticity of her authorship.

The case he makes, and makes best, is that Berners has always been a legend, devised and promulgated by historians of the English language and printing. When anglers came along looking for their past and found their first hero, ready-made, complete with obscure authenticity and vague, romantic uncertainty already in place, already well established with a certain amount of scholarly credence, in the character of Dame Juliana, they accepted her enthusiastically.

In the 1984 edition of *Trout,* Ernest Schwiebert states that a British angling historian, J.J. Dunne, pinpointed Berners' birth as March 16, 1383, which would have made her pretty old when *The Boke of Saint Albans* was first printed, and impossibly 114 years old in 1496 when *TFA* was included.

On the other hand, there is plenty of evidence that points to the existence of *TFA* at least as early as 1450, and possibly earlier still. The first quarter of the fifteenth century has been mentioned. McDonald, who has done the best and most recent investigative scholarship, places the writing of *TFA* between 1406 and 1420. It survives in a copy transcribed in 1450 and in *The Boke of Saint Albans* published in 1496. Apparently, both were derived from a now lost original.

So what comes down to us as history is a ready-made hero of suitably obscure origins, a person obviously of grace and education; of uncertain career and occupation — if indeed she was a "she" at all — who has presented the first written description of fishing with rod and line.

In *A History of Fly Fishing for Trout,* John Waller Hills probably sums up the dilemma best. After pretty thoroughly dismissing her from responsibility for *TFA,* he goes on to state,

"I shall treat her as author until a better claimant appears, for it is awkward to have to cite an anonymous book."[6]

And so shall we.

So what do we learn of fishing, once we've accepted that Dame Juliana is as close as we are going to come to an author for the time being? What does she have to offer?

What we learn first of all is that once we accept Juliana as the author of *TFA*, we have to recognize that she is at best an accurate reporter of the state of the sport at the time she lived and wrote. Fishing did not spring full-blown from her pen, nor did she describe a set of procedures that then caught on with the sporting crowd. What we find in *TFA* is the description of angling as it was practiced in the mid-fifteenth century, not an innovative directive on how it was to be practiced.

In fact, there is really little in *TFA* that describes how the fishing was done. What is well described is the tackle that was in common use, how to acquire it, and, of course, a dozen artificial flies that would still fish well today. The fishing information is sound enough that *TFA* went through 16 editions or reprints in the hundred years that followed its appearance, either as part of *The Boke of Saint Albans* or by itself. It was pirated ruthlessly by writers in subsequent centuries, and this can be traced right on through Walton.

Numerous reprints of the original exist, including replicas in blackletter, but if it is information you are after, the translation from the Middle English done by John McDonald and Sherman Kuhn and published in *Quill Gordon* in 1972 is tough to beat. It is at once well enough translated to be accessible and entertaining and well enough annotated to be instructive and leave the reader with a feel for the tackle and techniques of the day. They also retain the language of the time, so you feel like you are reading the real thing.

The *Treatyse* begins with a general prescription for a good and long life, the most vital aspect of which is "good and honest sports and games in which a man's heart takes pleasure without any repentance."

Of course, Berners knows that angling is the best sport going, but within the formal structure we've discussed, she's compelled to describe, and then discount, hunting, hawking, and fowling. Each for sound reasons is found less than adequate — which leaves fishing with the angle-rod as the prescription for happiness.

The key to angling, she explains, the first door which must be opened to enjoy the benefits of this good and honest sport, is the making of the tackle.

Heat-treating and multi-piece hollow construction were both familiar techniques in the rod-building of Berners' time.

The rod of the fifteenth century as she describes its construction was a three-piece model around 18 feet long.

A six-foot butt of hazel, willow, or ash was cut between September and the end of January. Heated and straightened, the shaft was next hollowed so the second and third rod sections could be stored inside.

The second section of the rod was to be of white hazel, half the length of the staff, and the third section of blackthorn, crabtree, medlar, or juniper, the same length.

The top two sections could be stored in the staff, which was capped with a spike that also served as a removing device for the stored sections. The staff was ferruled at each end. To fish, the second section was tapered to fit four or five inches — a handbreadth — into the small end of the staff. The third section was spliced to the second, probably overlapped and wound over with silk. Six horsehairs twisted together were wound round the tip section from the splice to the tip and finished with a loop for attaching the fishing line.

There follows a set of recipes for dyeing the horsehair to be used as line, with a prescribed color for each season or each type of water. Recommended are green for summer, yellow for fall, russet for winter, black for sluggish waters, and tawny for heathy or marshy waters.

Following dyeing, of which there are ample instructions, including dyestuffs, mordants, and cooking instructions, are the instructions for making lines of the dyed hairs. To facilitate twisting and plaiting the hairs, Berners recommends a mechanical device, of which there is an illustration. Joining the sections of the assembled line with a water knot, a taper is created and a line made that can then be attached to the loop at the end of the rod.

This rod was designed to be fished with a fixed amount of line. Generally, the line was the same length as the rod, though this would be one of the things that would change over the next two centuries.

The fly reel in Europe was still a long way in the future, so the method of playing hooked fish required the angler to deal with a fixed length of line and tire the fish with that. To this end, Berners offers sound advice: "If you can avoid it at all, do not let him go out on the end of the line straight from you, but keep him always under the rod."

With a fixed length of line, this is the only way a fish could be subdued, by bringing the bend of the rod into play to tire it. With the rod well bent and the fish under the rod, shock and pressure would be absorbed by the bend in the rod and not the line. The performance required of the rod dictated the type of wood most suitable for rod-building. Suitably limber and forgiving materials were necessary, and these were the qualities of the wood recommended for the middle and tip sections.

Hookmaking is likewise described thoroughly. Hooks at this time had to be manufactured from needles, and most anglers, it appears, made their own.

The process was quite simple: Heat the needle and allow it to cool, then raise the barb with a knife, bend it, flatten and file smooth the end of the shank, then heat it again and quench it to temper it.

Lines were snelled to the hook shanks, and the instructions provide a method of fastening leader to hook shank that we could use today, if we needed to:

The line is wrapped with thread where the end of the hook will lie, then the line is laid along the hook shank and the thread wrapped down the shank, binding the line to the hook. Two thirds of the way down the shank, the tag end of the line is doubled back over the wraps, and that is wrapped down. The end of the thread is passed through the loop in the end of the line twice, the loop of line is wetted, then pulled tight, catching the wrapping thread and pulling it under the wraps along the shank.

Berners, while the first major contributor to fly-fishing literature, was not strictly a fly fisher, nor was she strictly a fisher of trout. She includes a list of species native to England and advice on how heavy a line, that is, how many hairs, to fish for each of the species. Her list begins with one hair for minnows through 15 hairs for salmon. Trout and grayling required nine hairs, "great trout," 12 hairs.

Bear in mind that the pound-test of a horsehair, as researched by Al McClane, averaged 1.3 pounds.[7] This would scale Berners' trout tippet at just under 12-pound test, and almost 16-pound test for "great trout."

The balance of *TFA* is concerned with a lot of information that has little or nothing to do with fly fishing, such as different rigging and floats and sinkers. Berners discusses lots of different types of angling and a lot of outdoors lore related to fishing, as well as baits, rigs, and sundry stuff, all interesting, but contributing nothing to the lore of the fly.

Perhaps the most significant and lasting contribution *TFA* makes to the literature and practice of fly fishing is in the description of 12 fly patterns — "the XII" — that carry the angler through the year: the Dun Fly, another Dun Fly, Stone Fly and a color variation, Yellow Fly, Black Leaper, Dun Cut, Maure Fly, the Tandy Fly at St. William's Day, the Wasp Fly, the Shell Fly at St. Thomas' Day, and the Drake Fly. These flies were to be with the literature for hundreds of years; in fact, they are still useful patterns, and their styling would be resurrected in the Swisher and Richards no-hackle revolution of the 1970s.

In concluding *TFA* Berners entreats the angler to have manners and be a credit to his sport. Trespassing and poaching are eschewed, and a whole set of ethics is established for the comport of the angler, to keep peace with others and prevent causing trouble. Look to any of our modern books today, and you'll find the same type of advice in conclusion. Chances are that these days the advice is to release fish, join a conservation organization or be considerate of other anglers on increasingly crowded streams, or any number of points of style and etiquette that speak for the times. The specifics of the advice are less important than the fact that it is given. Still, the structure that first appeared in medieval France dominates our sporting books.

When considering the structure of fishing books, all things flow backwards, and *TFA* is our most remote touchstone in the past, where we find the origins of the structure we're accustomed to.

Insofar as equipment was concerned, *TFA* was thorough and useful. The building of tackle, the hooks, rods, and lines, could be accomplished today according to those instructions, and we could probably catch a fish with the equipment, too. Indeed, it has been done.

Berners, however, was not a caster. As we can see by her recommendations for nine hairs for trout fishing, she was not even a particularly light tackle angler. As modern as much of her advice seems, there is quite a bit missing.

Streamcraft is in some evidence. Berners recognizes that good places to fish include "wherever the water rests by the bank and the current runs close by and it is deep and clear at the bottom."

She knows the best seasons to fish and offers a good and sound list of conditions to avoid.

And while there is some practical advice on playing fish, there is no mention of presentation of the artificial fly.

It's coming, but it will require some time. Obviously quite a bit of time. It would be two centuries before Cotton came along to describe presentation. We'll meet him when he contributes to Walton.

As it stands, Aelian described the problem, then Berners gave us the rudimentary tool to begin to solve the problems of fly fishing.

OVERLEAF: *Dame Juliana Berners' fly, Black Leaper, and an 1889 etching of Izaak Walton, advocate of her patterns.*

CHAPTER THREE

IZAAK WALTON, BAIT FISHING, COTTON AND HIS CRONIES

If Aelian first presented the problem and Berners offered the technical solutions for the day, then Izaak Walton surely defined the angling lifestyle. *The Compleat Angler,* published in 1653, would become one of the most important and long-lived books ever printed in English.

Walton was born in 1593 at Stafford, northwest of London. The River Dove flowed near his birthplace, but it was London where things were happening and where Walton lived during his working years. His trade as an ironmonger (at least, he belonged to the Ironmonger's Company) evidently escalated him into gentle society, and he appears to have been a major player in London and church society when he baled out of urban life to the countryside where he would spend the rest of his life.

Intimate of John Donne, Dr. Henry King, and Sir Henry Wotton, he kept a good and literate circle of friends, and though he buried two wives, Walton seems to have lived a thoughtful, serene life in the midst of troubling political times. He died at age 90 and is buried in Winchester Cathedral beneath a stained glass window inscribed with the closing words of *The Compleat Angler:* "Study to be Quiet."

Though perhaps not quite the "bucolic loafer" he has been called, Walton was nonetheless well fixed when he left London behind and schlepped off to spend the rest of his life fishing the River Dove and contemplating the pastoral magic of the English countryside. He had plenty of time, the means and demeanor to reflect on life, sport, and nature, and if he was less than the consummate fly fisherman of his day — and he was — he can be excused. As we've learned from Norman Maclean, Walton was a bait fisherman and an Episcopalian. But even at that, his contributions to English literature and on angling in general are irrefutable.

The Compleat Angler, first published in 1653, is one of the most widely circulated books ever printed, not too far behind the Bible. It could well have been about any recreation and its charm would still have well carried it through the centuries. As it is, angling was the perfect vehicle for Walton's oft-imitated and never-matched style. The beauty of the English countryside, the rhythms of the weather, and the flow of the river and time attuned to natural cycles all form the canvas across which he paints his perceptions of the well-ordered life and the joys of sport.

Fly fishing per se occupies little in the early editions of *The Compleat Angler* — Charles Cotton added the fly-fishing material later — but somehow the book remains a vital part of our sport's history.

The Compleat Angler has been through hundreds of editions since it was first written. The various editors themselves have made significant contributions to fishing literature in the process of introducing and editing Walton. Witness the entrance of Dame Juliana Berners on the scene through John Hawkins' introduction to the 1760 edition of *The Compleat Angler.* And one of the first and finest essays on fly fishing comprised the first American edition of Walton. We'll be dealing with that when it comes along later.

Walton has truly been the locus for many innovative thinkers and writers on fly fishing. Because he has for so long been the campfire they all danced around, the study of his various editions, as the various editors made their own contributions, gives us an accurate perspective on our own history: cultural, literary, and piscatorial.

There have been several books written on the various editions of Walton, and these catalogue studies themselves are tough to find and expensive to buy. There's a full-time job here, let alone a hobby, so if you intend to keep fishing, be warned you are treading on dangerous ground when you take up Walton for a hobby.

Even the best intentioned of fishermen or casual historians is likely to get hung up at this point along the fly-fishing timeline.

Arnold Gingrich warns, "Good men have been known to get lost in the nearly four hundred editions of *The Compleat Angler,* never to be heard from again."[8]

The evidence is everywhere.

Ernest Schwiebert in discussing Walton gets bogged down and no longer is talking about trout, as his title promises, but instead wanders off on a perusal and analysis of seventeenth-century English politics, the Royalists and the Roundheads under Cromwell, and a whole host of things he picked up at Princeton University, picking through the stacks in the library and the brains of the professors. It all offers testament to Ernie's erudition, but really leads nowhere. But he's not alone. It happens to plenty of people.

For some reason the same affliction attaches to everyone who embarks on a discussion of Walton and his writing. The stuff is just that good.

It's a common reaction, once you've gotten hold of a copy of *The Compleat Angler* and begin to read it and place it in the perspective of angling history.

You can spend weeks wallowing around in this stuff and end up staying up so late at night trying to track down one writer's quotes in the copies of old angling books you suddenly find yourself unable to do without that you are too tired in the morning to get up and go fishing. Not that there is anything wrong with that, except that it has nothing to do with fishing.

Except when you deal with Walton. Perhaps that is the key. In Walton everything has to do with fishing, from the gleam of dew on the meadows, to the scent of wildflowers in the air, to the loves and pure life of the milkmaid. Where to sleep at night, what companions to join along the stream, and what's for dinner are all critical on a par with the quality of the fishing. In fact it seems the catching of fish was the least of Walton's concerns.

When he chose to illustrate a point of instruction, he simply caught a fish and proved his point. That's that, now let's make sure we have a good bed and a good meal for the evening. There is nearly as much poetry and singing in here as there is fishing, and in the end it is irresistible.

For all the overblown romance of his approach, it is Walton's wonderment in the natural world around him that is so enchanting. Newcomers to Walton are often surprised by the structure Walton took on in writing *The Compleat Angler*. The first surprise is that it is in dialogue.

The book begins with three characters — Piscator the angler, Viator the hunter, and Auceps the falconer — walking the Lea Valley from London to Hoddesdon. As the inherited structure dictates, the conversation introduces the three principal field sports of the age. Each character soapboxes on the superiority of his particular sport. Auceps discourses on birds and the element he trades in, that is, air; he is followed by commendation of hunting and its element, Earth, by Viator; and at last this character gives way to Piscator, who of course discourses on water, "the eldest daughter of the Creation, the Element upon which the Spirit of God did first move, the Element which God commanded to bring forth living creatures abundantly."

In this discourse we find the first evidence of Walton's enchantment with the natural world, and his gullibility and willingness to believe whatever is fantastic and marvelous about nature.

Piscator regales his companions with tales of rivers and fish, at once fantastic and incredible. Rivers he describes that turn red the wool of sheep that drink from it; rivers that dance when music is played; and a river that runs for six days and rests on the seventh.

No less miraculous are the different fishes he tells them of, fish that take up two acres of ground, fish two hundred cubits in length, and eels thirty feet long that come together in great writhing balls.

"The waters are nature's storehouse, in which she locks up her wonders," he explains.

He speaks of cuttlefish that cast forth a long gut out of their throat, like an angler doth his line; he speaks of the Adonis, a loving and innocent fish; and he provides testimony of both lustful and chaste fishes. As Du Bartas describes the Sargus in Walton:

The Adult'rous Sargus doth not only change
Wives every day in the deep streams, but (strange)
As if the honey of Sea-love delight
Could not suffice his ranging appetite,
Goes courting she-Goats on the grassy shore
Horning their husbands that had horns before.

In order that there remain a balance in the natural kingdom, Piscator describes, by the same author, the Cantharis.

But contrary, the constant Cantharis
Is ever constant to his faithful Spouse
In nuptial duties spending his chaste life,
Never loves any but his own dear Wife.

Carrying on like this leads to speculations that this may
be the first mention of what in modern times is to become
the legendary and much-maligned fishwife. Didn't I say this
stuff was irresistible?

To summarize the story line, Piscator and Viator take leave
of Auceps early in Chapter I. Piscator agrees to accompany
Viator the next day and take part in an otter hunt. There follows a spirited hunt behind the hounds, in which the otter is
killed, found to have recently whelped, so the pups are tracked
down and killed, too, just as enthusiastically. The killing is
done joyously, and Piscator explains, "I am (Sir) a brother of
the Angle, and therefore an enemy to the Otter: for you are to
note, that we Anglers all love one another, and therefore do I
hate the Otter both for my own and for their sakes who are of
my brotherhood."

There's a stark contrast to be found here between the wonderment he discovers in nature and the utter obviousness of
the righteousness in slaughtering otters because they are the
natural enemies of fish. But the slaughter is an exciting bit of
action nonetheless, another perfect end to a perfect day in
Derbyshire.

Once the family of otters has been dispatched, the cheer-
ful party retires "to an honest Ale-house where we may have
a cup of good Barely-wine, and sing Old Rose, and all of us
rejoice together."

The following days, and the remainder of the text, belong
to fishing. Viator has agreed to enter under the tutelage of
Piscator and learn the art of angling. In so doing, the reader is
instructed along with the devoted student.

To understand Walton is to understand the philosophical bent that has been attendant to civilized anglers since the beginning. Walton waxes endlessly on the beauty and wonders of nature — however misplaced his faith in legendary creatures and rivers — because the very nature that formed the backdrop of the pastoral lifestyle was for Walton the heart and soul of the fishing, the mystery and wonder of life. This is part of his charm, and one of the reasons he has lasted as long as he has.

Walton's protagonist, Piscator, the teacher, and Viator, the student, dialogue their way through *The Compleat Angler* like a meander through a meadow, and when he needs to illustrate a point, Piscator catches a fish by way of illustration.

In between is a whole lot of stuff that is a whole lot of fun to read.

It's important to recognize that Walton's technical contributions, the first-hand information he imparts, have to do with baitfishing and instruction in angling for the various species that inhabited the rivers and lakes north of London — chub, grayling, salmon, pike, carp, bream, tench, perch, eel, barbel, gudgion, roach, dace, and loach.

Walton was hardly original, but he was the best of his time. Between Berners and Walton are half a dozen surviving books, and each of these owes a considerable debt to *TFA*. Likewise each is well represented in the first edition of Walton, which was published in 1653. In case you care to pursue them, they are *The Arte of Angling,* 1577; *A Booke of Fishing with Hooke and Line* by Leonard Mascall, 1590; *Certaine Experiments Concerning Fish and Fruite* by John Taverner, 1600; *The Secrets of Angling* by John Dennys, 1613; *The Pleasures of Princes* by Gervase Markham, 1614; and *The Art of Angling* by Thomas Barker, 1651.

According to Hills, Mascall was the link between Berners and Walton, and he cites this as evidence: Mascall copied

Berners' list of flies, but four of them he names incorrectly. In all four of these cases, Walton repeats the error. Markham also differs slightly from *TFA*, but where this discrepancy exists, Walton follows Mascall.[9]

By the time Walton published in 1653, there had been some changes in angling practice, technique, and equipment since Berners first described the equipment. Casting was in its infancy but had been acknowledged as a part of the process of catching fish. Eyed hooks had appeared, and reels were not altogether unknown, though still not common, and certainly not for trout fishing.

Walton was in fact not much of a fly fisherman. His tackle was relatively heavy compared to many anglers.'

> *Let your rod be light and very gently; I take the best to be of two pieces, and let not your Line exceed . . . three or four hairs at the most, though you may Fish a little stronger above in the upper part of your Line: but if you can attain to Angle with one hair, you shall have more rises and catch more Fish. Now you must be sure not to cumber your self with too long a Line, as most do: and before you begin to Angle, cast to have the wind on your back, and the Sun (if it shines) to be before you, and to fish down the stream; and carry the point or top of your Rod downward; by which means the shadow of your self and Rod too will be the least offensive to the Fish, for the sight of any shade amazes the fish, and spoils your sport, of which you must take great care.*

So it appears that in Walton's time as well, anglers were always attempting to cast too much line — more than they needed to fish and more than they could effectively handle. Not much has changed in that respect. And they still prefer to position themselves so the wind is at their back, even though casting has changed considerably.

In Walton's day, the wind at your back carried the line and the fly over the target, where the fly was allowed to drift over the fish's lie. This technique came eventually to be known as dapping, but in Walton's day, it was *the* technique for delivering the fly. When the wind was strong, of course, the line needed to be laid on the water to anchor it and to allow the fly to drift over the fish.

While the wind was a consideration — in fact, for effective fishing a bit of a breeze was essential — it could also be troublesome. By way of advice, that the wind not keep the angler off the water, Walton quotes Solomon: "He that considers the wind shall never sow."

We'd say today, the best time to go fishing is whenever you can get away.

For fly fishing and fly dressing, Walton was beholden to Thomas Barker.

According to Walton himself, his 12 patterns were the rule of the day for anglers, but even at that, common fishing practice seems to have interpreted the prescription loosely for best results. It's notable that in the following passage Walton is at once admonishing the angler to pay particular attention to local insects and to imitate them for best results. At the same time, he advised that the 12 flies handed down from Berners are but a rough guideline.

> *That whereas it is said by many, that in flye-fishing for a Trout, the angler must observe his 12 several flies for the twelve months of the year, I say, he that follows that rule, shall be as sure to catch fish, and be as wise, as he that makes Hay by the Fair days in an Almanack, and no surer; for those very flies that used to appear about and on the water in one month of the year, may the following year come almost a month sooner or later, as the same year proves colder or hotter: and yet in the following Discourse I have set down the twelve flies*

that are in reputation with many anglers, and they may serve to give him some observations concerning them. And he may note that there are in Wales and other Countries, peculiar flies proper to the particular place or Country; and doubtless unless a man makes a flie to counterfeit that very flie in that place, he is like to lose his labour, or much of it; but for the generality, three or four flies neat and rightly made, and not too big, serve for a Trout in most rivers all the Summer.

No sooner does he finish up discussion and instruction in the art of dressing flies than he enters into an explanation of how to fish natural flies baited on a hook. Izaak Walton was an incorrigible bait fisherman.

COTTON AND THE TRUE PATH

Walton's great contribution to the literature of fly fishing came when he invited his friend Charles Cotton to contribute to the 1676 edition of *The Compleat Angler.*

Cotton was 37 years Walton's junior. Born and raised at Beresford Hall in Derbyshire, Walton probably knew Cotton when he was growing up and developing his reputation as a fly fisher.

Cotton was to the manor born, and though he suffered at times for means, he was of the gentry. His writing, it seems, served to occupy his time and offset the boredom of having little to strive for once the fishing season was over. Known as a mild pornographer, he didn't have to take too many things seriously. Lucky for us, fishing and deadlines meant a great deal to him.

Cotton explains in the introduction to Part II of *The Compleat Angler*, "Being Instructions How to Angle for a Trout or Grayling in a Clear Stream," that he found himself with less time than he supposed and wrote the entire piece in 10 days. Not bad for what many consider the finest book ever written on fly fishing.

Cotton couched his instructions in the same dialogue form Walton used, though his prose nowhere approaches the excellence of the old man. But then, Walton couldn't hold a candle to Cotton when it came to fly fishing, either. They were paired well, each considerably adept where the other was deficient.

It is in the contribution of Cotton that we begin to pick up some dedicated fly-fishing information. Piscator again attends Viator's desire to be instructed, and he takes him to Cotton's famed fishing house on the Dove.

This stone cottage with its slate roof still stands on a small peninsula that is formed by a bend in the River Dove. Above the door the two sets of initials overlaid — C.C. and I.W. — the same as adorn the frontispiece of Cotton's Part II of *The Compleat Angler,* still offer testimony to the friendship and literary collusion of these two. In the garden of the fishing house, at the stone table that still adorns the grounds, Piscator leads his student Viator down the road of fly fishing with advice and information that today are astounding for their accuracy and insight.

This is an orderly instruction, progressing from a description of tackle, a discussion of the rudiments of streamcraft, to the dressing of artificial flies, and finally a tour of the Dove, complete with some fish-catching.

The tackle of the day was a rod 15 to 18 feet long, length determined by the size of the stream. He describes the best as made at Yorkshire, from six, eight, or 12 pieces smoothly spliced with silk windings. The length of the line was prescribed as a yard or two longer than the rod, and it was explained this length of line was no handicap to an angler adept at handling tackle, except in "woody places and in landing of a Fish, which every one that can afford to Angle for pleasure, has some body to do for him, and the length of line is a mighty advantage to the fishing at distance; and to fish *fine, and far off,* is the first and principal Rule for Trout Angling."

This "fine and far off" business is one of Cotton's best known and most often quoted lines.

With this remark we know at once who we are dealing with; an angler who is smitten with his own casting, the mark of a true fly fisherman modern in all respects.

While the practical angler Walton advised to keep the line a reasonable length, it seems the longer the better when we deal with Cotton. It may well be this is the beginning of the school of thought still with us today, that if we could only cast 10 feet farther, we'd catch more fish. This 10 feet is standard, no matter how far the cast. A man after our own hearts! Now we can begin to relate. I can trust an angler who always wants to cast farther.

Casting was truly on the threshold of becoming an angling technique at this time in fly-fishing history. Cotton has decided the best line is one that tapers steadily from the rod to the fly, and he understands the taper is important for both accuracy and a gentle presentation. Yet anglers of the seventeenth century still were required to fish with the wind. If that wind were strong, then a portion of the leader on the water served to anchor the fly. Otherwise, the presentation of the fly was primarily what we now know as dapping, described earlier in this chapter. The cast as we know it and the drag-free float would come later, as tackle changed and made these techniques possible.

Tippets for Cotton consisted of two strands of horsehair attached to the hook, with three above, then four, five, six, and so on until the desired total length was achieved. The length of the sections of course was dependent on the length of the strands of horsehair available.

The number of sections may have varied, but Cotton was firm on the two-hair tippet, and this is another of his well-known lines: "He that cannot kill a trout of twenty inches with two, deserves not the name of angler."

This is a pretty stiff requirement for the name of angler, even in our day. It would have been more so in Cotton's, when the angler had no reel, and no spare line. The fish would need to be subdued with the flexibility of the rod and the strength of the hairs. A 20-inch trout, then as now, would run about three pounds. Individual strands of horsehair, of the kind Cotton preferred, tested just over a pound in strength. So his criterion dictated the skill to land a 3-pound trout on a 2 1/2-pound tippet.[10]

At this writing, that would mean landing a 3-pounder on 7X-tippet — certainly not unheard of these days. More to the point, perhaps heard of too much. Any angler who today lands such a fish on a tippet that fine is going to be talking about it to anyone who will listen. We've all heard the stories. There are plenty of such catches about, but it's still a good fish on light tippet, and we have the advantage of graphite rods and fine reels.

Cotton provides instructions for fly tying that can still be followed today, and the conversations between Piscator and Viator have been repeated thousands of times since this writing, the only change occurring in the grammar and delivery. The sentiments and observations are current, now as in Cotton's time.

When Piscator opens his dubbing bag, he proclaims, "I will make no scruple to lay open my Treasure before you," to which Viator replies, "Did ever any one see the like! What a heap of Trumpery is here! certainly never an Angler in Europe has his shop half so well furnisht, as you have."

Truly, it's a modern enough scene and dialogue to make us blush, those of us with our own heap of Trumpery.

Fly-dressing instruction is well given, step by step. The north-country style Cotton describes favors slim, sparse dressing, presaging by two and a quarter centuries the Catskill style in America; whereas the southern streams around London exhibit fatter, fuller patterns, much like the western patterns of the 1970s would later favor. Cotton makes severe fun of their crudeness, a prejudice that too would be repeated in twentieth-century American fishing.

Cotton advises choosing dubbing colors against the light of the sun, advice we will hear echoed by Skues and Leisenring in later centuries.

Walton's parroting of Berners' 12 patterns gives way in Cotton to that author's own list of 65 patterns that serve the angler throughout the year.

And lest we forget why we're on the stream at all, there follows a recipe for trout that still sounds good today. This ends the fly-fishing information in Cotton's Part II. In order that his instruction fulfill the promise of his title, he describes bottom fishing for trout and grayling, but there is no more fly fishing here. Nor does there need to be. A new era has been opened.

Along with Cotton, Thomas Barker and Robert Venables were also instrumental in pushing fly fishing to a new level. One of these, Barker, Walton pirated for his information on fly fishing.[11]

The other two were in fact both contributors to Walton's first expanded edition in 1676. Cotton is the only one who has survived down through the centuries.

To certain copies of the fifth edition, which contained the Cotton addition and was the last edition printed during Walton's life, a Part III, "The Experienc'd Angler, or Angling Improved," by Robert Venables was added. The copies with Venables' contribution were entitled *The Universal Angler.* Venables was later dropped from the compilation.[12]

Venables is significant in the history of our sport because he was the first writer to discuss upstream fishing, so we can assume that at this time upstream fishing was pretty widely accepted as a successful practice. This is an important step in the evolution of streamcraft and fly fishing. It both takes advantage of changes in the tackle and dictates further refinement to come.

In fact, casting a fly upstream makes a significant marker in the course of fly-fishing history. It's a recognizable step on the way to modern fly-fishing practice.

John Waller Hills, the British fishing historian, in fact breaks the evolution of fly fishing into four distinct steps or developments he calls landmarks. These are: imitation, "the copying of the colour and shape of the natural insect;" presentation, "when action as well as colour and shape is copied, and the fly is cast in such a manner as to come over the fish in the same way as the natural insect does," meaning here, an upstream presentation; casting to individual fish; and finally all of the above developments "combined in the use of the floating fly."[13]

Berners covered the first landmark. Venables was the first writer to mention upstream fishing. Indeed, his description of the advantages and disadvantages of upstream versus downstream is scarcely any different from the same arguments today. Fish upstream and you tend to line your fish, so you must fish a short line, which works well, because a fish facing upstream is not likely to see the angler below it. Downstream, a longer line is needed, since the fish is facing you and you can easily amaze it.

James Chetham was the first to record fishing for individual fish, in *The Angler's Vade Mecum,* published in 1681. Though fishing to an individual fish is inherent in fly fishing, and certainly was commonly practiced, Chetham was still the first to write specifically about this approach.

While the surface fly was not unknown, the dry fly as we know it, Hills' fourth landmark, would not come along for two centuries.

It is necessary to continue to stress the difference between what is written and what is practiced. So far the history of angling has also been the history of English literature, specifically fishing literature. The two go hand in hand. Up until now we have writers who show us angling as it is practiced. This is not prescriptive fishing writing, but rather, descriptive.

Soon these will begin to overlap. John Waller Hills says of the seventeenth-century writers, "When we leave them we leave the reign of the book and come to that of the manual."

CHAPTER FOUR

RONALDS AND THE EMERGENCE OF ENTOMOLOGY

Enter the eighteenth century, a time which produced no great fishing writers. Thought and theory rest in peace for the next 100 years. Manuals, we find, define the written history of fly fishing in the eighteenth century, and while these may represent a dearth of good writing and thinking on angling, they are not altogether worthless. What manuals do, they do well, and that means providing information. With enough information we can conjure up a history of the angling itself. With knowledge of the tackle and procedures, we can imagine what it must have been like to use the gear, and hence, develop a picture of the state of fishing itself, as it was practiced decade after decade during this century.

For during this period there were changes in the tackle. The developments and advancement over the 180 years between Cotton and Stewart were significant, if not immediately dramatic.

"Advance followed advance by measured and orderly procession; we are hardly aware that we are traveling," the historian John Waller Hills observes, "and it is only when we have reached the end and look back that we are conscious of the distance which we have covered. . . ."[14]

"At its beginning [the eighteenth century], men fished much as they did in the fifteenth: at its close, everything that we have now was in use except the American split cane rod."[15]

The way we determine the changes that took place are by the descriptions in the relatively uninspired manuals of the time, strung out over nearly two centuries. During this time some significant advances came along.

If the literature of this time lacked inspiration, these times served well as a resting place for the past and a launching pad for the modern angling that was soon to follow.

First, let's take a look at some of the significant publications of this time, then at the tackle as it developed.

The first of the manual-style books appeared in the late seventeenth century, in 1681 when James Chetham published *The Angler's Vade Mecum*. Ernest Schwiebert calls this one "a curious mixture of plagiarism, shrewd wisdom and practicality, original and creative thought, and a credulous belief in witchcraft."[16]

Chetham borrowed Cotton's fly patterns verbatim, and then added a few of his own, but in doing so added nothing really original. Chetham did present a new concept, however — the concept of fishing to an individual fish. This is, you will remember, one of the foundations of modern fishing diagrammed by Hills, the third of his requisite steps toward modern fly practice.

The eighteenth century proper opens with Robert Howlett's *Angler's Sure Guide* in 1706. As was the order of the day, Howlett took facts and ideas from whomever he wished. His angling was just as typical of the time, and it is easy to relate to his method of casting wet flies down and across on a taut line, which he explains as keeping "your flie always in a gentle motion, that a fish may hang himself though you strike not."

Howlett also strikes an original note when he offers a bit of advice that anglers still have trouble learning: When you are unsure of seeing your fly, strike when you see a fish rise within reach of your rod and line. This is sound advice, and today when rods cast farther and trout demand smaller and smaller flies, we reach a point where almost all of us can cast a fly farther than we can fish it with certainty. This is evidently not a new problem. The solution is nearly 300 years old.

John Gay published a two-volume edition of pastoral verse, *Rural Sports,* in 1720, the best of which is devoted to fly fishing, and the best of that, unless you care to delve into the literature for its own merit, is perhaps this bit of verse, which appears in just about every reputable history ever written:

> *Around the steel no tortur'd worm shall twine,*
> *No blood of living insect stain my line;*
> *Let me, less cruel, cast the feather'd hook,*
> *With pliant rod athwart the pebbled brook,*
> *Silent along the mazy margin stray,*
> *And with fur-wrought fly delude the prey.*

While one of the better writers of the time, Gay lends little to the developing saga of fly fishing. This verse, however, offers substantial testimony that already was growing the kind of moral superiority among fly fishermen that still seems to be a character trait.

Perhaps the most significant writer of the eighteenth century was Richard Bowlker, who around 1747 ushered in a great deal that was new and modern. Richard was author of the first edition, and his son Charles took over subsequent editions of *The Art of Angling,* which stayed in print until 1854, a publication history unprecedented in any books besides *The Compleat Angler* and *TFA.*

The Bowlkers made some significant contributions: directions for fly fishing, including one of the first recommendations for fishing upstream; instructions for fly dressing; and its explanation of the natural history of aquatic insects, which surpassed anything published to this time.

Bowlker really cleaned house when it came to cataloguing fly patterns. He dispensed with Berners, Cotton, and Chetham and established his own list of about 30 patterns he considered important.

This was long overdue. The standard fly patterns had been altered, borrowed, pirated, and plagiarized for so long that many of them were no longer meaningful. They certainly bore little resemblance and little relationship to the natural insects they were originally meant to represent. Bowlker provided a cleaned-up list, one that was greatly simplified, and a collection of flies that was to give rise to the precise imitation and reliance on aquatic entomology that would reach its fullest expression in 1836 with Ronalds' publication of *The Fly-Fisher's Entomology.*

Modern fly dressing traces a direct lineage to Bowlker's instructions. Dressing instructions were clear and concise, flies dressed lightly, their delicate, spare style echoing the British north-country fashion. Bowlker created size by specifying hook sizes, and matched the naturals in terms of color, shape, and form.

Modern styles still echo Bowlker, like Leisenring and the Catskill school, with fashionably sparse and light dressings.

Bowlker's reporting of upstream fishing was reiterated by Thomas Shirley in *The Angler's Museum* in 1784, a growing practice that would spring full-blown upon the angling world in the work of Stewart, and eventually in the revolutionary approach of Halford and Marryat in the final days of the nineteenth century.

Cotton, Chetham, and finally Bowlker had established a firm foundation for modern fly fishing. Solid footing was now in place as the visionary developments of the nineteenth century opened to a new world of ideas.

Lacking inspired thought, then, what did the how-to style of this period tell us about the fishing?

In Cotton's time, just as the seventeenth century turned into the eighteenth, the standard weapon was a rod from 18 to 21 feet long. Cotton praised Yorkshire rods with fir butts, six, eight, or 12 pieces spliced together, and gracefully tapered. Hazel was a favored material, though some used cane with a hazel top, and whalebone was generally used for the actual point. Spey rods were still made with this same whalebone tip well into the twentieth century. Venables' favorite rod was four feet of hazel, two feet of blackthorn or crabtree, finished off with whalebone.

As early as 1620 ferrules were used in rods; in fact, Berners' original rod was ferruled, though splicing soon replaced the crude ferrules of her day. By the time of Walton and Cotton, rods were spliced for the season. As workmanship improved, of course, ferrules became more popular, and it's likely that as soon as they were dependable enough to prove advantageous, they were adopted. Splicing, no matter how carefully done, tended to work loose after extended periods of fishing. Still, it managed to hang on well into the nineteenth century until the craftsmanship of the ferrule made it the wisest choice.

By the 1700s, rods were no longer homemade. There were reputable suppliers and builders, offering tackle made to the standards and practices of the day. Thus could the angler concentrate on fishing and leave craftsmanship to others able to concentrate on it.

As commerce and transportation — and the British Empire — developed, rod materials changed. Native materials all but disappeared. Hazel and other varietal woods vanished, and lancewood, hickory from America, bamboo from India, and greenheart from South America took their place.

Sir John Hawkins' 1760 edition of *The Compleat Angler* mentions hickory. Greenheart appeared about 1841.

Rod guides were first described by Howlett in 1706. First came iron hoops on stems driven into the shaft of the rod. Later, rings lashed to the rod that lay flat when not in use and flopped up to carry line. The appearance of rod guides means reels were being used. There had to be line at the angler's end to pass through those guides, and which had to be stored on reels. Reels had been mentioned by Barker in 1651 for trolling, and by Walton in 1655 for salmon fishing. They weren't long in coming into trout fishing.

Lines were twisted horsehair or horsehair and silk mixed. Mostly 12 to 20 hairs tapered to one, two, or three. Heavy lines began to gain favor. They were far easier to cast and control than light hair lines. Silk and horsehair were often woven together, but these could be troublesome, as the materials stretched differently.

About this time there entered into the lexicon a material called "Indian Grass," or "Indian Weed," used as casting line — Hills writes that the first mention occurred in 1700, in the front of an edition of Chetham's *Angler's Vade Mecum*:

At the Sign of the Fish in Black Horse Alley near Fleet Bridge liveth Will Brown who maketh all sorts of Fishing-Rods and selleth all sorts of Fishing Tackle: also Charles Kirby's Hooks, with Worms Gentles and Flys: and also the East India Weed, which is the only thing for Trout Carp and Bottom Fishing.

The material was advertised to be strong, fine, and more invisible than hair or silk. It is commonly mentioned throughout the eighteenth century until superseded by gut. Hills is at a loss as to the identity, and so is the director of the Royal Botanical Gardens himself, who was unable to ascertain the nature of the mysterious material's origin.

Sounds rather suspiciously like something you could as easily smoke as fish with; in fact, both the names Indian Grass and Indian Weed seem pretty indicative of the nature of the material, especially in light of the fibrous qualities of Indian hemp. But I guess we'll never know. Maybe that's why there's so much trouble tracking down its identity. I might try a pipeful while I was trying it out for casting efficiency, if I could be sure I'd remember what I was doing. Far be it for me to speculate where the director of the Royal Botanical Gardens could make no progress.

Venables was the first writer to mention the gut line, a lute or viol string which seems to have cast well but soaked up water. Samuel Pepys remarked on gut line as well in 1667.[17]

The first reference to silkworm gut as a line material occurred in 1724, in *The Compleat Fisherman* by James Saunders. Gut came slowly to replace horsehair, and by 1760 it was still recognized as a new item in London, though its properties of strength and low visibility were well documented and touted.[18]

Cotton provided description of 65 flies, Chetham 20. South-country flies were fatter and bigger than the slim northern flies, which had just a bit of hackle and a short body. Each style was considered worthless, even laughable, beyond its home region.

The two schools of fly dressing were already set apart. Berners had introduced the accurately imitative. In Cotton's time came the general, impressionistic designs, the same theory that would produce the "fancy flies" in American fishing much later. Cotton's own patterns were strictly imitative, though the more general designs were in wide use. Venables, for instance, recommends "a light-coloured fly for a clear day, a red or orange fly for a thick water, a dark fly for dark weather, a black or brown fly for whitish water."

This was the tackle, then, that dictated technique, streamcraft, and angling strategy.

"Concealment was got not by kneeling or crawling, as we do, but by standing well off the bank, and throwing a long line, fishing, as Cotton said, fine and far off."[19]

For the most part, casting was still a downwind proposition. Certainly occasions presented themselves when an angler might cast a short line upstream, but it was a specialized situation. Likely more consistent success came from working down and across. Limp, long rods and horsehair lines, later giving way to gut, made this necessary. The lines were made invisible by keeping them off the water. This is something every writer recognizes as essential. It was long after the seventeenth century before anyone cast into the wind.

The familiar mechanics of modern casting were not even approximated at this stage of the game. Mostly, the angler attempted to lower the fly onto the water and, by using the length of the rod and lowering it to adjust the amount of line that fell on the water, hoped to obtain a reasonable approximation of the drag-free float; or, by maintaining tension, draw the fly or flies over the fish. Other cruder methods of fishing allowed for a taut line, down and across, the flies in constant motion, as in loch fishing, which often called for a brace of wet flies kept in constant motion across the surface.

Flies were fished near the surface, but the true floating fly imitating the adult insect was still a long way off. It isn't hard to visualize this type of fishing. In fact, we are able today to fish like this, though we find it a handicap to attempt these old techniques with short, modern rods. Our style of casting was, however, technically impossible for the angler of the eighteenth century. Still, fishing managed to get done, and with success that differs scarcely from ours today.

With the wind behind him, catching the heavy part of the line, and the fine line of one or two hairs perhaps brushing the surface, the angler on the bank, well back and reaching downstream with a long, light, limber rod, could effect a pretty long and drag-free drift, as well as a down-and-across swing, classic wet-fly form.

Stewart, years later, reported anglers on the Tweed killing heavy baskets of fish using this same method, even when they had other techniques at their disposal. The old techniques still had their place.

"Thus do the great masters talk to each other across the centuries," commented Hills.[20]

Wading was a common practice, but since everyone waded wet, they probably avoided it whenever possible. It had to be pretty uncomfortable in all but the warmest months.

Prior to the era of Stewart and his upstream tactics, little fly fishing took place in the low-water months of summer. Their techniques made fishing more effective during higher, off-color — and colder — water.

As high summer would have been the comfortable months for wading, it must be assumed wading was not a particularly passionate, enthralling aspect of the sport.

William Scrope (pronounced *skroop*), author of *Days and Nights Salmon Fishing in the Tweed,* advises, as late as 1843, never "go into water deeper than the fifth button of your waistcoat." You should also examine your legs, he says — if they appear black or purple, get on dry land; if they are "only rubicund," no worry. Scrope must have been quite the intense angler. To wade through rubicund to black or purple would take concentration indeed. You'd think an angler would be aware his legs were turning rubicund, though by the time they had turned black, it might very well be necessary to look in order to determine if you had any legs at all, color no longer being a real issue.

Rudimentary equipment for wading was long in the future.

Though the equipment was crude, and tactics and techniques plodded along to match the development of the tackle, catches could be substantial.

Cotton reports 35 to 40 fish was an especially good catch from the Dove, where the fish average a pound or better. A bag of six trout and three grayling was considered quite respectable for a student of Cotton.

By the time the eighteenth century had turned into the nineteenth, Stewart considered a 10-foot rod big enough for any type of water. He stated he generally used one measuring eight to nine feet long. Hills states this reduction in length reflects anglers' increasing use of the reel, which made such a long rod unnecessary. Stewart was still ahead of his time, though, and long rods, from 11 to 12 feet, remained common. Hills himself says he started fishing with a 12-footer on the Test, the Itchen, and the Kennet. Hills would have started fishing in the late 1800s.

Stewart, writing in the middle of the nineteenth century, said a good fisherman should average 15 pounds of fish a day, and a great angler 20 pounds. Stoddart states 30 pounds was good on the Tweed, and not many attained it. John Waller Hills, writing in 1921, said at Cumberland Eden 30 years ago (which would put it about 1891) a good rod would do about 40 fish, not at all uncommon. Bags were not particularly heavy in Cotton's time — he makes complaint of poaching, and this may have to do with the fact that the bags weren't bigger than at the time of Hills, or even today.

This then was the state of angling itself through the eighteenth century. The nineteenth was to prove a different story. Just as the one century produced a lot of changes in hardware and not much in thought, so the latter saw a tremendous amount of activity in theory and approach.

Suddenly, bright, creative people were fishing, and writing about it again. And this time their writing was typified by new ideas as well as a systematic organization of the odds and ends of the past couple of centuries, the possibilities exposed by the development of more efficient tackle.

The same countryside that inspired Walton and prompted Cotton to publish the initial codification of fly fishing gave rise to the revolutionary work of Alfred Ronalds 200 years later. The Derbyshire countryside a hundred miles northwest of London is a world apart from the legendary rivers south of London that we usually associate with the British tradition — the Itchen and the Test — but it is these northern streams that provided the fodder for a lot of the work that would come to define fly fishing as we know it.

By the middle of the nineteenth century, W.C. Stewart, from his vantage point on the banks of the Tweed and the Scottish tradition, on the border 200 miles north of Derbyshire, would codify and define the upstream style that, coupled with Ronalds' entomology-based theory of imitation, would give us our modern approach and open the door for Marryat and Halford and the dry-fly revolution.

RONALDS BRIDGES THE GAP

The first significant landmark in the nineteenth century was the work of Alfred Ronalds.

Ronalds established a reliance on observation, intellect, and science that remains a standard in fly fishing. While he was not the first to base imitations on real flies, he was far more thorough than anyone before him.

Ronalds was a talented aquatic biologist and illustrator, and these talents meshed perfectly for the publication of his landmark *Fly-Fisher's Entomology* in 1836.

Between 1836 and 1856, over a period of 20 years, Ronalds completed the bridge between the practice of angling and the science of entomology, giving the artificial fly a description and a definition rooted in taxonomy. He was the 1800s' earliest writer of note, and the archetypal scientific angler.

He created scientific angling. It is impossible to overstress the importance of Ronalds.

Ronalds' fly catalogue totaled 47 artificial flies. Since he illustrated both the artificial fly and the natural insect it represented, his illustrations totaled 94. In his gorgeous illustrations, the form and color of the dressed flies mirror so closely the natural insects that they are nearly indistinguishable. Through his illustrations we see instinctively what imitation is all about. Sporting theory meets artistic practice.

Ronalds' particular success came in creating the union between angling and entomology. Establishing a direct relationship between the name of the artificial fly and the Latin taxonomy of the living insect, he did what no one had really ever done before — he provided a reliable and accurate method of distinguishing one artificial fly from another, and exporting that imitation to wherever it might be useful.

His descriptions and recommendations for particular flies were repeatable, simply because they were correlated to a scientific identification.

In retrospect this is one of those discoveries that seems like no big deal. Coming as we do at the art of imitation, fully aware of the scientific basis for our imitation, it is hard to imagine that this wasn't always so.

Genius is often described as one who grasps the truth just a little sooner than everybody else, and in this case, it's a fitting description of Ronalds' particular genius.

You might say he took the obvious and recognized it.

Until Ronalds made the connection, artificial and natural insects both were described by color and size. The same vernacular name served for the live insect and the imitation.

Just as brilliant was the way he marketed his new approach to imitation. Flies were identified by the common and vernacular names of the artificial, with the Latin identification at all times subservient to the more usable moniker. He casually linked the well-known artificial with the natural, and presto, before anyone had a chance to object — which they invariably do to anything new and original — the art of angling had become fused with the science of imitation.

Ronalds' contribution was not restricted to taxonomy alone. The sum and total of scientific streamcraft based on trout behavior took great strides forward under his methodical investigations.

From his observation blind on the Blyth in Staffordshire Ronalds developed thoroughly new models of trout feeding lanes and holding lies. The science of refraction and a trout's vision appear in his writings, and his analysis of the trout's window into the world above is as accurate and accessible today as it was when he developed it. Theories put forth by Ronalds would be reiterated and confirmed in additional research lasting well into the twentieth century.

Indeed, in Vince Marinaro's 1976 publication, *In the Ring of the Rise,* the author reproduces Ronalds' diagrams and explanations on refraction as a basis for dealing with the world from the trout's point of view.

Technically accurate, and yet entirely accessible to the non-scientist, i.e., the angler, his work drew little from his predecessors and almost nothing from his contemporaries. It is this originality that has given his work such staying power. Ronalds has only recently been eclipsed as an authority on British hatches, and this by men following his model, with updated observations on hatches throughout Great Britain.

STEWART LOOKS UPSTREAM — AND TAKES A FEW CASTS

The next great leap forward came in 1857 when William Stewart published *The Practical Angler.*

From the border lowlands of Scotland 200 miles north of Derbyshire, the swift rivers produced a school of angling that would prove to fill the third of the four required landmarks on the road to modern angling as prescribed by John Waller Hills. This third step was the predilection for fishing upstream.

Stewart explained in his book that the art of fly fishing consists of knowing 1) what to fish with, 2) how, 3) when, and 4) where to fish.

In Stewart's own words: "The great error of fly-fishing, as usually practiced, and as recommended to be practiced by books, is that the angler fishes down stream, whereas he should fish up."

This infatuation with upstream fishing had a tremendous effect on the theory and practice that would follow, filling the role of both precursor and catalyst for the already-dawned and soon-to-be-imminent dry-fly revolution. As acceptance of Stewart's ideas grew, it was an easy step to the purism and dogma that would come to angling across the Atlantic into North America and well into the twentieth century.

The upstream school didn't originate with Stewart — he simply reported the practice as it was adopted by a growing number of anglers. Not more than one in a hundred anglers fishes upstream with the fly, according to Stewart, yet reluctance to do so, he maintained, was the greatest impediment to success in clear waters. The angler has little problem catching a few trout in off-color water, Stewart explains, but when the water is low and clear, the traditional methods of fishing downstream yield little but scared fish.

The reasons for fishing upstream are presented thoroughly and clearly. When Stewart is finished making his case, it's tough not to be a believer. The reasons are, like most great angling discoveries, pretty evident in retrospect: The trout doesn't see the angler; there is a much better chance of hooking the fish when the fish rises above the angler; fishing upstream disturbs the water less than fishing down, especially when a fish is hooked, as it is then played through water that has already been fished. Fish hooked by fishing downstream are played through the water the angler has not yet fished, and consequently, the fish he hopes to catch are spooked by the fight of the one hooked. Last, the angler can much better adapt the action of his fly to imitate the action of the natural insects when the cast is made upstream — that is to say, a drag-free drift is better achieved on the slack line that results from the upstream cast. In short, his arguments are a concise statement of all the things we swear by in dry-fly fishing.

Even though these are the very methods the purists on streams south of London would soon adopt, along with a rapid devotion to the dry fly, Stewart stops short at creating a rigid dogma. In fact, when he describes the flies he feels are best to fish, he surprisingly emerges as a proponent of the impressionistic school, preferring a fly that only generally resembles the natural. He feels it very unlikely that a trout can determine the precise color of an artificial fly. Anglers "scrupulously exact" about the color of the fly proceed to draw the fly across the water "in a way in which no natural insect was ever seen moving," he reasoned.

Stewart instead stresses the shape of the fly, preferring the sparse, lightly dressed style typical of the northern rivers of England. He also feels a fine gut leader is essential to success, but above all, the way in which the fly is presented is paramount in its acceptance by the trout.

He is firmly in the corner of Presentation — as opposed to Imitation — as the most critical aspect of fooling a trout, and this is quite consistent with his expostulation on upstream casting. This emphasis on presentation over imitation was not without opposition, however. But Stewart meets the controversy head on, putting it away neatly, as is his style in building a case for all his theories.

The opposition, Francis Francis — who was, incidentally, in the midst of the dry-fly proselytizing and PR work that provided the foundation for the throne of purism to which Halford would soon ascend, hailed as the original cat's pajamas of angling — took a swat at Stewart's theory, claiming it a provincial quirk, rather than a sound theory. Here's Stewart at his best as he rises to that occasion.

The opinion that it is necessary to imitate the particular fly on the water at the time has recently received the weight of Mr. Francis Francis' support, who in advocating what may be called the English theory gives a sort of side-swipe to Scotch anglers — the drift of his remarks being, that though a small assortment of flies may do well enough in Scotch streams where little fishing goes on and anglers count their takes by the dozen, it will not answer in the much-fished streams on the other side of the border, where anglers count their takes by the brace. If Mr. Francis' views as to an exact imitation being necessary in English streams be correct, which we very much doubt, he will require to find some other reason for its being unnecessary in Scotland than this. In comparing the severity of the fishing in Scotch and English streams, it must be borne in mind that the former are, as a rule, open to the public and that the latter, as a rule, are preserved and fished only by a favored few. If Mr. Francis will point out any stream in England, in which he thinks it worth while to throw a fly for trout, that is more and better fished than Tweed and its tributaries, we shall be very much surprised. And on behalf of Scotch anglers we repudiate with scorn the bare idea that it requires less skill to catch a Scotch trout than an English one, or that the former in any way receives an inferior education as regards flies, etc, to his English brother. In fact, we believe that in the before-mentioned streams the education of the inhabitants is as superior to that of the inhabitants of English streams as the education of the

people of the one country is admitted to be to that of the other;
and supposing the most accomplished believer in the English
theory — ay, even Mr. Francis himself — engaged on a mile
of Tweed along with twenty or thirty Galashiels weavers (by
no means an unusual number), we question if his basket at
the finish would illustrate very strongly the superiority of his
theory and practice.

In repudiating the precise imitation theory, Stewart not only makes a strong case for the sophistication of the Scottish trout, but also the education of the Scottish people. How Francis replied to this reaction we don't know, but he would have had to have been a big fool to pick up the gauntlet and go rod-to-rod with 20 or 30 Galashiels weavers on their home water. Stewart is a class act in his defense of the practice he advocates, and at the same time, the tradition of public water, the prowess of the common man on the stream, and the literacy and education of his country.

Nothing that Stewart said, however much sense it made, would have been any good without tackle to carry out his theories. It is critical once again to realize, if we are to understand the history of angling and not just the history of the literature of fly fishing, we have to look at the tackle and project ourselves, with our skills and knowledge, onto that time, onto those streams with that equipment in our hands. Thus do anglers communicate across the centuries.

Tackle in the time of Stewart was achieving a level of sophistication that allowed the angler, for the first time, some choice in where he would cast. Downwind was no longer compulsory.

Tapered lines, either horsehair or the mysterious Indian Grass, and silkworm gut leaders were the rule of the day, as they'd been around long enough to be in common usage. By the middle of Stewart's century, rods and their capabilities had changed a great deal. Hickory was well established as a rod-building material. Bamboo, commonly called cane, was in wide usage and according to John Waller Hills, Stewart favored a whole cane butt and middle with a split cane top. The first rod built entirely of split cane appeared in Great Britain between 1830 and 1840.[21]

These cane rods were not the six-strip American invention. That would come later. However, the advance in materials did provide for a wider variation in the way the fly was presented. In short, the angler was able to cast, at last, without relying strictly on the wind for accuracy, distance, and fly placement. Thus it's with a great deal of relief that we come across, at last, some casting instruction from Stewart.

> *When the line is thoroughly soaked, take the rod in your right hand, raise it with sufficient force to make the line go to its full length behind, and then pausing for a moment till it has done so, with a circular motion of the wrist and arm urge the rod forward, rapidly at first, but gradually lessening the speed, so that when it stops no recoil of the point will take place. The whole motion of the rod in casting should be in the shape of a horse-shoe; and care must be taken not to urge the flies forward, till they have gone the full length behind, or you will be apt to crack them off.*

With casting instruction out of the way — which also includes the importance of landing the fly on the water before the line and the necessity of keeping the rod high, above 45 degrees, in order to turn the line over — Stewart next makes a bold move. He admonishes the angler never to fish a long line when a short cast will do. Fishing a long line, he says, is "a natural consequence of fishing down stream" and an essential one. But accurate upstream fishing favors the short cast, and for the first time in 180 years, fishing "fine and far off" is only a conditional bit of advice. We'll hang on to it because it certainly has its place, but Stewart has pretty much banished it for the time being as restrictive and specialized.

His insistence on the advantage of the short line carries over to playing fish, too. The short line gives better and more instantaneous control, whether it be of the fly or the fish, and is to be preferred always.

Stewart offers a wealth of sound advice, not entirely without a sense of humor and enjoyment, things it pays to revisit. Fish as if you expect a rise at every cast, he advises. "We have lost many a good trout in an inadvertant moment."

"If you are tired, or the trout are not taking, sit down and console yourself in some way or other. A late writer upon the subject suggests, that for this purpose the angler should carry a New Testament in his pocket, to which there can be no possible objection, but we rather think most anglers prefer spiritual consolation of a very different sort, coupled with sandwiches; there is a time for all things, and at noon we must admit having a preference for the latter method."

OVERLEAF: *Butcher, a trout and salmon fly invented by G.S. Jewhurst of Tunbridge, Kent.*

CHAPTER FIVE

HALFORD AND SKUES: THIS CHALKSTREAM AIN'T BIG ENOUGH FOR THE BOTH OF US

From the north-country streams of England came the most lasting landmarks in the development of the fly fishing. The idylls of Walton and the technical prowess of Ronalds and Stewart originated north of London, but it was the streams south of the city, the Test and the Itchen, that would be the settings of the most controversial developments the sport has ever seen — indeed, a controversy that would carry right to our own fishing today.

The birth of this controversy coincided innocently enough with the emergence (ahem!) of the dry fly under the divine leadership of one Frederick Halford and culminated and matured with the development of the artificial nymph under the sponsorship of G.E.M. Skues. Both men added to our literary history with writings on their opposing positions.

Frederick Maurice Halford was the first genuine dry-fly snob. In fact, he gave the character type its definitions. Between *Floating Flies and How to Dress Them,* published in 1886, and *The Dry-Fly Man's Handbook,* published in 1913, Halford developed from a progressive theorist with a better idea to a dogmatic pedant who believed anyone who fished differently than he shouldn't be allowed near moving water, let alone fish for trout.

He brought the art of dry-fly fishing to a high art, then drew a line in the dirt.

Of course, whenever any man draws a line in the dirt, another is certain to come along and step across it, whether as an act of defiance or because that line happens to lie across the other man's path. Such a second man was George Edward MacKenzie Skues.

Skues' writing was thoroughly grounded in fly dressing, and his game was the sunken fly, or nymph.

The two schools, Halford and Skues, and the wealth of literature and angling expertise their ideas spawned, provided one of the lasting and constant conflicts even in the ranks of American anglers today. There's scarcely a fisherman who won't side with one or the other at any given time over the superiority of the floating versus the sunken fly. The ongoing philosophical conflict forms an ideological core within the sport.

The same conflict that erupted on the chalkstreams of England carried to the New World. And Americans in their way came to their own reckoning with the two philosophical approaches.

Dry-fly fishing no more sprang from the mind of Halford than upstream casting from the pen of Stewart. Rather, a long and winding history prompted the overriding importance of the floating fly to the exclusion of all other methods. There was a long and developing history of the floating fly that led up to its ascendancy in the sport. Certainly there were plenty of references to floating flies throughout the written past of fly fishing.

George Philip Rigney Pulman is generally credited as the first to write of the dry fly in *The Vade Mecum of Fly-Fishing for Trout,* published in 1841. By the time the third edition was published in 1851, Pulman had added a paragraph discussing the "line switched a few times through the air to throw off its superabundant moisture."

From about 1840 on, flies were being fished dry all over the place. Over the southern Hampshire chalkstreams, the Itchen and the Test, the Devonshire Axe, Pulman's home water, the Wye in Derbyshire and north to the Tweed in Scotland the dry fly flew. Before long it was the established method on southern chalkstreams, though it came to the Test a bit later than other rivers. By the 1860s, the dry-fly method was well established on the southern streams. From 1880 onward it was the only way to fish.

This purist dogma owes a great deal to Frederick Halford, though the essential elements were already in place.

Arnold Gingrich put it succinctly when he stated, "Purism, which it would not be too fanciful to say was fathered by Stewart's upstream technique on the body of Ronalds's entomology."

One of the earliest chroniclers of the dry fly was Francis Francis — the same one who sideswiped the trout of Scotland and rose Stewart's ire — who upon taking the helm as angling editor of *The Field* in 1857 reported the dry-fly method then beginning to capture the hearts and minds of the chalkstream crowd. But the champion above all champions of the floating fly was Halford.

Frederick Halford's first book, *Floating Flies and How to Dress Them,* appeared in 1886. In it he begins to chronicle the work of George Selwyn Marryat, who was regarded as the finest angler on the southern chalkstreams, and Henry Hall. Hall was an engineer who worked closely with Marryat and developed the process and metallurgy capable of producing the eyed, light-wire hooks appropriate to dressing the revolutionary dry flies that were developing.

The development of the eyed hook was fairly important. No longer was a fly finished once its snelled gut wore out. The eye also afforded the angler with some choice in the size of tippet, making it possible to match different fishing conditions. Connection of tippet to hook was solved by a regular on the Itchen, Major W.G. Turle, whose knot provided a rigid connection to the fly and helped settle it on the water in the desired cocked position.

Halford in concert with Marryat did a lot of work developing the fly that would ease the fishing on the difficult streams of the south where a gentle presentation was so critical. The hard-enamel-finish silk lines had supplanted horsehair by this time, but they too presented problems all their own. Stiffness, chipping, and lack of sensitivity and response were the biggest shortcomings. They did allow the angler latitude in casting direction but were nothing compared to the response and efficiency of oiled silk — especially an oiled silk line with a woven-in taper.

Working together, Halford and Marryat developed the first tapered lines, forerunners of the modern double-tapers, and continued to improve the manufacture and production of silk lines for many years.

Halford's first two books (*Dry-Fly Fishing in Theory and Practice* came out in 1889) are considered his most valuable. The more he wrote, the more he became mean-spirited and intolerant of any but the most precise upstream imitative style of dry-fly fishing. Halford came to view all chalkstreams as distinctly dry-fly water.

"If he is to be criticised it is because like most reformers he overstated his case. He considered that the dry fly had superseded for all time and in all places all other methods of fly fishing, and that those who thought otherwise were either ignorant or incompetent," says Hills in his discussion of the dry fly, in *A History of Fly Fishing for Trout.*

Before the end of his life, Halford had seen the development of the dry fly become a system, a method of fishing that spread around the world, wherever trout were found, and he'd had a lot to do with that distribution. Even on streams with their own dominant methods, it had become an option in the arsenal of trout fishermen. It had also become a religion in the south-country rivers where it was spawned. Halford was the link through which the dry fly came to America, too, through Theodore Gordon, about which more later.

In spite of Halford's pedantry, he changed fly fishing for the better. The changes wrought by his chronicling the work of Marryat brought some of the biggest changes of all time to fly fishing. And while the dogma of the dry fly was eventually to crack and allow a more diverse approach, a more reasonable, well-rounded angler to emerge, the development of dry-fly technique changed the face of angling forever, and it changed it for the better.

With the full weight of the fishing world behind his dry-fly advocacy, it's no surprise Halford felt like his tail had been badly twisted when a young upstart on the Itchen they shared devised a method of fishing different from his and published a book about it.

Codified as it was, the dry-fly method had become one-dimensional. No longer did the method answer to specific problems that had once needed solving; rather, it extracted a slavish devotion from anglers. With its institutionalization, the upstream, imitative dry-fly method had developed to where it answered only its own demands for self-vilification. It was time for the sport to grow again, move beyond the gospel according to Halford.

It was G.E.M. Skues who appeared to champion the sunken fly, the nymph. And he did this on the same Itchen whose waters Halford had deemed approachable only through the moral and ethical superiority of the dry fly.

Skues published his *Minor Tactics of the Chalk Stream* in 1910, three years before Halford published his last book (*The Dry-Fly Man's Handbook*). In it he described what we know today as nymph fishing.

Skues began his own brand of angling revolution as gently as can be imagined. He opens with ample credit to Halford, relating his early experiences with nymphing trout as though he chanced into the phenomenon purely by accident. As complimentary as he is of the dry-fly ideology, he plays it as though he were trying to be good but somehow the fates conspired against him to make him catch selective fish on a sunken fly instead.

"In those days, with 'Dry-Fly Fishing in Theory and Practice' at my finger's ends, I began with the prescription, 'Pink Wickham on 00 hook.'"

Skues would have us believe he was a determined dry-fly man who accidently on several occasions, several years apart, happened to catch fish with a dead-drifted sunken fly, when the only hatch-matching pattern left in his book proved to be dressed with low-grade hen hackle: unfloatable, though he might try to put it dry over a bulging fish.

Shortly, though — in fact, by the time the first short chapter comes to an end and the second begins — we have Skues fishing and describing three stages of an aquatic insect hatch: The emergence of the nymphs, the dry-fly dun stage when trout feed on the surface, and the end of the hatch, when trout once again feed subsurface on the "broken submerged fly," as he puts it.

This last stage we know now as the stillborns, or perhaps the spinnerfall, which will be discovered again in the last half of the twentieth century.

There's a symmetrical poetry to be found in Skues, in the description of how he fished a Greenwell's Glory to nymphing trout, creeling four of them before

it seemed to fail of its effect, though the river was freely dot-
ted with rings, and after wasting much time I tumbled to the
situation, and changed to a floating No. 1 Whitchurch — most
effective of Yellow Duns — on a cipher hook. The effect was
immediate, but I had put off too long, and when I looked up
from basketing my third trout to the Whitchurch the rise had
petered out. But I was not done yet. I changed to a Tup's Indis-
pensable dressed to sink, and, fishing upstream wet in likely
runs and places, I made up my five brace before I knocked off
for lunch.[22]

That's fishing a hatch!

John Waller Hills in *A Summer on the Test* places Skues in
an interesting perspective. Hills himself, astute scholar of
angling history that he was, throughout his angling career was
immersed in his times, from about 1890 through the first
decades of the twentieth century. His perspective is from the
midst of the conflict that surrounded the storied chalkstreams.
Hills also traced the history of fly fishing through the four
landmarks we have been watching, and once the dry fly came
on the scene, Hills had no more historical criteria to be filled.
He had outlived his own history, which is always a concern
when we try to find a continuum in our own experience with
our history.

> *When, exactly twenty years ago, Mr. Skues wrote* Minor
> Tactics of the Chalk Stream, *he effected a revolution. The*
> *dry fly was at a height of its intolerant dictatorship, and the*
> *other method was discarded and ridiculed to such an extent*
> *that enthusiasts of the school of Halford regarded Mr. Skues*
> *as a dangerous heresiarch. Much water has flowed under the*
> *bridges since then, and in that water many are the trout which*
> *have been caught on a sunk fly which would not have fallen*
> *to a dry. More and more each year does nymph fishing be-*

come a part of the modern angler's equipment, and he who does not possess the art is gravely handicapped. And at the same time has come the realization that this art is both difficult and delightful. It demands different qualities and it makes a different appeal, it opens a new field of observation and experiment, and it is as exacting a process as the other, for upon my word I find trout harder to catch under water than on top.[23]

Though Hills ceases to be useful, it is big of him to acknowledge the limits of his own historical outline. Coming this far with him has been enjoyable and instructive.

Minor Tactics even today reads smoothly, seducing with its easy theory and execution, and there is inspiration here for anyone who casts a fly. Surely it struck the anglers of the day the same way, for with its publication, the pendulum began to swing back away from the dry-fly purism that had swept Great Britain, heading towards a more balanced approach to our ever-evolving sport. It ushered in the model of the all-round angler that Francis Francis envisioned in 1867 when in *A Book on Angling* he wrote:

Now, there are two ways of fly-fishing, viz. with the dry fly and with the wet fly. Some fishermen always use one plan, others almost as pertinaciously use the other. To use either of them invariably is wrong. Sometimes the one will be found to kill fast and sometimes the other.

Skues had been fishing for well over 30 years, in the chalkstreams of England and throughout Europe, before he published *Minor Tactics*, so his studied informality and wonder at his pretended inadvertent discoveries must be seen as just that. Skues was far too bright and original a thinker otherwise to fool the reader for too long with his charade.

His second book, *The Way of a Trout with a Fly,* offered an expansion on the earlier, broad strokes taken in *Minor Tactics* 11 years before. The later work is a thorough compendium of chalkstream methods, including wet flies, dry flies, and nymphs, all theory and technique polished and gleaming, presented within the easy familiar style that makes Skues so enjoyable even today.

It's hard not to quote Skues, as his lucid, fluid passages echo a sensitivity, clarity of thought, and Victorian elegance that are irresistible.

Here's an essential, however, on the frontispiece of *The Way of a Trout with a Fly.*

When the wise man laid it down that there were three things which were too wonderful for him — yea, four which he knew not — he came to the climax with "the way of a man with a maid." Some future Solomon will end with a fifth — the way of a trout with a fly — for it combines the poise of the eagle in the air, the swift certainty of a serpent upon a rock, and the mystery of the way of a ship in the midst of the sea, with the incalculableness of the way of a man with a maid. Our aviators seem to be on their way towards a solution of the way of the eagle in the air. The mystery of the way of a ship in the midst of the sea has yielded all its secrets to the persistence of modern man, but the way of a man with a maid and the way of a trout with a fly remain with us to be a delight and a torment to thousands of generations yet unborn.

By the time he published *Nymph Fishing for Chalk Stream Trout,* Skues had begun to take himself a bit too seriously. His earlier brilliance was tarnished in his last book, by his insistence on taking Halford to task on every point of disagreement. He cited chapter and verse, and carefully refuted each point — something that hardly needed to be done in 1932, when nymph fishing was well established and respected and Halford had been dead for a quarter century.

This is too bad, for before he lapsed into this pettiness, excusable though it may be, Skues contributed a great deal of original thought and instruction to our sport. By his own admission, Skues felt that nymph fishing was simply another avenue to streamside success — not an exclusive approach, and it certainly required the accompaniment of good dry-fly technique.

> *The indications which tell your dry-fly angler when to strike are clear and unmistakable, but those which bid a wet-fly man raise his rod-point and draw in the steel are frequently so subtle, so evanescent and impalpable to the senses, that, when the bending rod assures him he has divined aright, he feels an ecstasy as though he had performed a miracle each time.*[24]

Skues was not without his own prejudices, however. The British insistence on fishing to feeding trout was extant in his writings, and he makes a point of explaining that he maintained strong principles when it came to fishing the water. It was essential, Skues maintained, to cast to feeding fish, the nymph or dry fly, whichever most closely matched what the fish were feeding on. Fishing the water was just not done. It would surface later, in America, where boorish practices went unrecognized.

The vision of trout and the effect it has on the way in which they react to the fly and the angler; fly dressing; the importance of caddis hatches; the sinking and floating portions of the tippet — reading through Skues for the first time, if you have been fishing for any time at all, is like reading your most basic understandings of the sport reiterated from before the time you were born as an angler.

Most of what we use is here. Many of the things we have discovered for ourselves we find Skues discovered before us. And of course, the same magic we find in modern nymph method held Skues in its grasp. His instructions for the use of a marrow spoon to extract the contents of a trout's stomach and the inspection of said contents on a white china plate is an approach that would be with us for far too long into the twentieth century. It later reappeared as the trout stomach pump, which, while it yields sound information, is a bit intrusive to the minds of many anglers. It's a personal issue — but Skues was right there on top of it in his last book.

The mystery and subtlety in the way a trout took a nymph was a constant fascination to Skues:

> *Oh, thrilling the rise at the lure that is dry,*
> *When the slow trout comes up to the slaughter,*
> *Yet rather would I*
> *Have the turn at my fly,*
> *The cunning brown wink under water.*

is just a single stanza of a poem that carries on like this for some eight double stanzas.

Before we move on there's a little matter of this man's name. Here's how Don Zahner chose to immortalize the unusual pronunciation:

> *There was a nymph angler named Skues,*
> *Whose doctrine brought nothing but "phooeys."*
> *Now he fishes for haddock*
> *From his tussocky paddock*
> *To let the "old boys" know just who he's.*[25]

The groundwork of nymph-fishing theory laid by Skues was built upon by many, but principal among them was Frank

Sawyer, the riverkeeper on the Avon north of Salisbury. Sawyer was widely recognized in Europe for his expertise in fishing small nymphs. It was Charles Ritz, son of the famous Swiss hotelier, who brought him to the world's attention — but we'll be meeting Ritz later in this history, from the other side of the Atlantic.

At this point it's a bit overdue that we pay a visit to North America, where already the traditions of fishing a new continent are well under way. To get in on the beginning of this, we have to move back a few steps in time, as the British angling tradition through the Skues years overlaps a period during which fly fishing was going through its own changes in the United States.

Far more important than a precise chronology of development is an understanding of the weft and weave of the fabric of tradition against which the excitement and adventure of North American fishing were played out.

The British traditions were well established, and they were not without their own severe dogma. Many of the rules, especially the rules of the hallowed Hampshire waters, were not even a consideration to the Americans. The British tradition, where we leave it, made specific demands on the angler. Codes of conduct and expectations of behavior, concepts of propriety on the English chalkstreams are quite foreign to the American tradition.

Consider: On the beats of the Hampshire streams, the anglers even today fish to rising fish. Fishing the water is thought less than civilized. Getting in the water is deemed equally as boorish. Carefully manicured, the chalkstreams are absolutely never waded; rather, rising fish are fished from the bank once they have been observed feeding on the surface. The dry fly is used preferentially — even today it is a more aristocratic approach — and only when that brings no result is the upstream nymph brought into play.

The British terminology "killing" a trout is not to be taken lightly. It is generally accepted that once a trout is caught, it's groceries. Return a trout to the river and it becomes a bottom-feeder. As such it'll never be caught again, because anglers on these streams never fish on the bottom.[26]

Feeling a bit stifled, a bit constrained in your fishing? Let's pack our bags and cross the Atlantic where fly fishing gets a new start on fresh waters.

OVERLEAF: *Fancy fly Parmachene Belle.*

CHAPTER SIX

NEW WATERS, A NEW LAND: THE RISE OF AMERICAN TRADITION

American fly-fishing history has traditionally been tough to track down prior to the Civil War. There were few landmarks to note the development of a peculiarly American fly-fishing tradition. The magazine work of Frank Forester is notable; the Bethune edition of Walton's *Compleat Angler* and Thaddeus Norris' *American Angler's Book* of 1864 were the most significant publications chronicling the development of our sport. These pretty much lead us up to Theodore Gordon, who alone among American anglers has inspired a true religion, and drawing on the best of the British tradition, was to enshrine a distinctly American angling in the Catskills.

According to some historians, there was no sportfishing to speak of prior to the first half of the nineteenth century. But bits and pieces emerge, giving hints that there was some fishing going on, and it was pretty good, too.

These bits and pieces indicate that recreational fishing was pretty well established as early as the middle of the eighteenth century. Paul Schullery in his fascinating history, *American Fly Fishing,* offers some reasons why there seemed to be so little going on for so long. No fishing books were written in America until the nineteenth century.

There are a couple lines of thought on this.

The overriding religious philosophy that ruled the public life of colonial America in the early days tended to stress the pious and productive pursuits over the recreational and fun. Well into the 1700s, religion dominated what small amount of publishing there was.

Certainly there was plenty of fishing — there just wasn't a lifestyle built up around it yet.

Schullery put it in a way we can well understand:

> *But the shortage of published works on fishing is poor evidence; historians, were they so sarcastic, might point out that this is about the same as assuming that because nobody published books about sex in America before the 1800s, nobody was engaging in it. Fishing, like sex, was not a publishable topic.*[27]

Other evidence is available, besides books, that fishing enjoyed some wide acceptance. Journals, laws preserving public waters and access rights, retail price sheets, and artwork all indicate there were time and inclination for leisure sports, and fishing was chief among leisure and recreational activities.

If we wait until an identifiable literature of fly fishing comes along to document the sport, we have fallen victim once again to confusing history of fishing literature with the history of fishing itself.

In the 1800s, writes Schullery in *American Fly Fishing,* the British officer-sportsman was a standard and recognizable character in America. Thus the appearance of Sir William Johnson, Royal Superintendent of Indian Affairs in the American Colonies, who, according to Ernest Schwiebert, fished the Kenyetto near the Adirondacks following the French and Indian Wars, around the year 1775.

He built a fishing house on that river — on Sacondaga Lake, according to Schullery. Schwiebert says it burned and he built another, called the Fish House by local trouters.

Whether or not Johnson was a fly fisherman is speculation. There has been more of this than historical fact when it comes to Johnson, but that's the way history works sometimes.

At any rate, there are various allusions to fishing for bass, for tidewater trout, and for char throughout the 1700s. It is certain that sport was found in fishing. Philadelphia had several fishing clubs. The Schuylkill Fishing Company was established in 1732, and several others sprang up in the following 50 years. Advertisements from the time indicate tackle was widely available.

The British presence in Canada at that time no doubt had a great deal to do with the development of salmon fishing, and we have to assume that fly fishing was fairly common and well known, if not yet widespread.

A price sheet supplied by George Lawton, tackle-shop proprietor, lists plenty of gear that is easily identifiable as fly tackle. The sheet was supplied in 1803, along with an invoice and filled order shipped to Meriwether Lewis who was preparing for an extended trip with fellow officer William Clark. Clark's tackle, it appears, wasn't fly tackle, but the equipment was available and in use at that time.[28]

EXPLORATIONS AND FIRST CASTS

American fly fishermen became much easier to study once they began writing more, which happened in the early 1800s. Out of necessity we have to briefly fall back onto the literature of fishing as a substitute for the history.

By 1829 the market was right for the first American sporting journal, *American Turf Register and Sporting Magazine,* but fly fishing was only a tiny adjunct to the coverage. However, it was enough to offer glimpses of the fishing that was going on, and the center seemed to be the Letort, Silver Spring, and Big Spring in southern Pennsylvania. And while local developments, techniques, and fly-pattern adaptations were most certainly in evidence, the tradition was, without a doubt, decidedly British.

Not until the middle of the nineteenth century was there any definite appearance of a growing departure from this British identification.

The best tackle was still imported from England, but by the middle of the century, equipment that rivaled the British was being manufactured in America.

Tackle catalogues indicated that flies were in common use for a variety of species.

Arnold Gingrich, expert on angling literature, believes the earliest American written history of fly fishing may be the 1833 *Natural History of the Fishes of Massachusetts, embracing a practical essay on Angling.*[29]

So we take what we can get, and what we get is pretty good when it comes to George Washington Bethune, who edited the first American edition of *The Compleat Angler.*

Published in 1847, there was nothing notable about the publication of Walton in this country — few books, as we know, have had the reprint history that Walton has enjoyed, and for all the right reasons, too — but what was significant about the American edition was the addition of a tremendous amount of information about how fly fishing was conducted in America, the earliest complete essay on the subject to appear in this country.

John McDonald, who published the entirety of Bethune's essay in *Quill Gordon* — handily saving us the difficulty in coming up with the Bethune edition of Walton — reminds us also that Bethune was restricted to using wet flies on brook trout. Though in England enthusiasm for the dry fly was begun, we're a long way from England now.

Brook trout were the native fish in eastern streams. Brown trout have yet to be imported, and rainbows are still a western species.

This doesn't mean that American angling was without controversy or choice, and this is the first thing Bethune takes up, what he calls the two schools: one which insists on imitating the insect the fish is feeding on, and the second which relies on presentation rather than imitation. Bethune places himself in the second school. The trout in America, he explains, lack the sophistication of their English brethren — and in the case of waters that have never seen a fly, which he says the American fly fisher sometimes meets with, "the trout, if fairly on the feed, will take anything that is offered to them."

Still, a reading of this essay furnishes ample evidence that trial and error were the keys to successful fishing, and Bethune claims that as the summer wears on, his flies grow smaller. Even untrammeled waters held trout that exercised a native caution reflecting water level and clarity. Concluding, Bethune offers 15 fly patterns, among which "the experienced angler will recognise some old and highly valued acquaintances."

"Frank Forester" was the pen name chosen by the Englishman Henry William Herbert who came to America in 1831. Writing under the pseudonym relieved him of the responsibility of having lowered himself to write in *The Spirit of the Times*, an important magazine of the day. Forester is not particularly well regarded by historians with any sense of literary appreciation, though George Reiger calls him "America's first great outdoor writer."[30]

Forester appears to have been running from something when he moved to New York. His father paid his debts, but young Herbert was still prevented from coming home. Herbert wrote historical, romantic novels, which paid well enough, but when he began writing racing and fishing stories, his career really took off.

Edgar Allen Poe is quoted as saying, "[Forester] has written more trash than any man living with the exception of [Theodore S.] Fay."[31]

Forester's books — *The Warwick Woodlands, Fishing with Hook and Line* — comprised stories which had originally appeared in *The American Turf Register,* the leading sporting periodical of the day. His *Frank Forester's Fish and Fishing,* published in London in 1849, and New York in 1850, was the first completely original American book on fishing.

Forester's contribution, while controversial in terms of literary merit, nonetheless served an important function in American angling history. It separated the methods and intent of sportfishing as opposed to commercial fishing. In all cases, Forester preferred the qualities of saltwater fish over fresh — yet, he was a confirmed fly fisherman whenever it served to catch fish. It's interesting to note that, in the past decade of renewed interest in saltwater fly fishing, one of the first angling writers the country produced should have been a confirmed saltwater fly fisherman.[32]

Forester contributed an essay on brook trout fishing in Long Island streams to the Bethune edition of *The Compleat Angler.* Most notable in this essay, aside from the fact that brook trout abounded on Long Island, is Forester's no doubt imported sense of superiority. "I would not give a sixpence to kill the finest trout that ever ran line off a reel, with a groundbait, and even spinning a minnow I hold ignoble sport, as compared with throwing the fly."

Forester admits that the American trout tolerate heavier tackle and larger flies than the fish on British waters, but concedes the "distinction is growing smaller every day," and "where in consequence, finer tackle and greater skill are constantly coming into requisition."[33]

TOWARDS AN IDENTITY

It was not until 1864 when Thaddeus Norris published *The American Angler's Book* that Americans had a definition of a native style of fishing.

Norris proclaimed an outlook and philosophy of angling as democratic as any ever, anywhere. Had he been writing in sixteenth-century England, he probably would have even said a few nice things about falconry and hunting. His live-and-let-live outlook defined a few character types of fishing, types to avoid, such as the Snob Angler, "who speaks confidently and knowingly on a slight capital of skill or experience"; the Greedy, Pushing Angler, "who rushes ahead and half fishes the water"; and the "Spick-and-Span Angler, who has a highly varnished rod, and a superabundance of useless tackle" whose display of catch at the end of the day "depends much on the rough skill of his guide."

These are just a few of the types Norris runs down, and they are all types we know and recognize, perhaps all too well. The True Angler, Norris' archetype, is an image of the self-reliant, innovative, capable, sure American, the same who forged into the frontier, founded a new nation from nothing, and killed him a b'ar when he was only three. He is the angler we all want to see when we look in the mirror.

Here he is in Norris' own words:

A modest man; unobtrusively communicative when he can impart a new idea; and is ever ready to let a pretentious tyro have his say, and good-naturedly (as if merely suggesting how it should be done) repairs his tackle, or gets him out of a scrape. He is moderately provided with all tackle and "fixins" necessary to the fishing he is in pursuit of. Is quietly self-reliant and equal to almost any emergency, from splicing his rod or tying his own flies, to trudging ten miles across a rough coun-

try with his luggage on his back. His enjoyment consists not only in the taking of fish: he draws much pleasure from the soothing influence and delightful accompaniments of the art.

This is the stuff of invigorating tramps through rugged hills, of the simple, nourishing "hearty breakfast of mashed potatoes, ham and eggs, and butter from the cream of the cow that browses in the woods," before the angler sallies forth to find "how exhilarating the music of the stream! how invigorating its waters, causing a consciousness of manly vigor, as he wades sturdily with the strong current and casts his flies before him!"

This is the angler who prepares trout cooked streamside for lunch, followed by a nap before the evening's fishing, far from the hustle of commerce and too-proper trappings of city life. This is the very stuff that makes up the view we have of ourselves as Americans, and Norris swaddles it in the clothes of angling.

While some of it smacks these days perhaps a bit too much of truth, justice, and the American Way, you have to admire anyone who can wade sturdily in cold trout streams while maintaining a "consciousness of manly vigor."

Norris is well aware of his sources — he knows the British traditions and developments, and his interest here is in codifying the American tradition as it was developing.

He makes some important pronouncements on tackle, too, proclaiming the single-handed rod the instrument of choice of those who have fished with it only a short time. The English version he proclaims far too heavy and cumbersome, and advocates instead a lighter version, and even seems to be hinting at some sort of progressive taper.

Flies, he explains, need not be numerous. Beginners are warned not to make the mistake of following the British tradition without modification. A limited assortment of the English flies is all that is necessary in this country, and "an extensive knowledge of flies and their names can hardly be of much practical advantage."

Fishing upstream gets the same dismissal. American streams are fast, he says, unsuited to casting upstream. "The force of the current in many a good rift would bring the flies back, and, as I have seen with beginners, entangle them in the legs of his pantaloons."

Ernest Schwiebert calls Norris both our Walton and our Cotton; Arnold Gingrich, on the other hand, claims he virtually worships Theodore Gordon, whom he'd "call our Cotton, in counterpart to the role of Thaddeus Norris as the American Walton."[34]

However you choose to enshrine him, Norris offered us a picture of ourselves as peculiarly American anglers that we took to heart and cling to even now.

VIRGIN WATERS

Throughout these early days, the stream that repeatedly surfaces in the writing, literature and snippets, is the Brodheads, though the Pocono rivers were also accessible to Philadelphia and New York, where the majority of recreational anglers were most apt to make their living during the week. Prior to the Civil War, however, there was plenty of exploration going on, from sea to shining sea. Lewis and Clark had traversed the country, after all, in the first decade of the nineteenth century.

It's not surprising that the limestone country of southwestern Pennsylvania provided a standard of angling, as well as a jumping-off point for the more adventurous traveler with a rod. By the middle of the century the Poconos, the Catskills, and the Adirondacks were seeing a steady and growing parade of anglers. Transportation was relatively easy up the Hudson and Mohawk valleys. The Adirondacks were still pretty wild, while the Catskills were already heavily logged by the 1840s. As early as 1840 and certainly by 1864, the immense brook trout of the Rangeley region of Maine were well known, and well used by stillwater, big-fish anglers.[35]

The Pacific Northwest, Michigan, Colorado, Nebraska, Utah, and Montana had all been fished with flies by 1860. The Yellowstone plateau had been fished with flies by 1870. Sports writers were hyping Colorado by the 1860s; in 1865 the Michigan grayling was identified and acknowledged — by 1900 it would be extinct.[36]

By 1870 most of the waters in the country had been fished. Exploratory angling was over. All sporting species had been identified, and while some remote waters had perhaps not seen a fly, the real pioneering was over. It was time to get down to business and seriously begin to fish these waters.

Regional fly patterns emerged, and while development and sophistication came earlier to the streams of the Eastern Seaboard than they would in the Pacific Northwest or the Mountain West, the process was both rapid and distinctive, a tradition that maintained the parts of European roots as were useful and invented the rest as needed. Development was under way, mining and logging were taking their toll, and American streams were no longer virgin waters. It happened that quickly.

The Brodheads in Pennsylvania occupied the first period of American fly fishing. However, its storied brook trout fishing was finished by the last decade of the nineteenth century, the cold-water habitat the unfortunate victim of logging and development.

The rivers of the Catskills, the Willowemoc, Dry Brook, and the Beaverkill; Schoharie, Delaware; Rondout, Esopus, and Neversink became the next wellspring of American angling. These rivers would become both the mecca and the laboratory for the next 50 years of fly fishing in America.

The Civil War, or rather the Reconstruction that followed it, makes a significant breaking point between the age of American exploration and the age of development. Part of this development was the single most important technical advance in tackle in the history of angling: the six-strip split-cane rod.

Details of the cane rod's development we'll handle later — suffice it to say that the split-cane rod made casting a reality — casting in any direction, without regard to the wind. This was a crucial element in the development of upstream fishing, and, consequently, to fishing the dry fly. Without the casting qualities of split cane, dry-fly fishing may well have been just another temporary sidetrack. The theory and the tackle are dependent on one another at this point.

It's also significant that at about the same time, the rivers of the East and Midwest were not only discovered, but suffered the first impacts of development, over-fishing, and environmental change that would alter the nature of their fisheries for good. Native brook trout, which populated all of the eastern rivers, depended on clear, cold water. Once logging began, this was the first thing to go. As mature timber was logged off, streams flowed dirtier and warmer. Brook trout fled to the cooler, cleaner feeder streams and the higher elevations, if they were accessible to the fish. Where they weren't, the diminished habitat simply determined the carrying capacity of the stream and populations adjusted themselves. Fish simply died out as proper habitat disappeared.

Logging was responsible for the disappearance of the Michigan grayling as well as the eastern brook trout. The final years of the century met with an altered fishery.

Rainbow trout, perhaps the most widely dispersed of the trouts, and a perennial favorite among anglers, were originally native only to California. From there they were shipped to virtually every corner of the world where there was habitat that suited them — in short, any place with clear, cold water.

Rainbow trout made the trip to New York in 1874 when Seth Green, working for the State of New York, received them at the hatcheries built at Cold Spring Harbor and Caledonia. In 1876, this same strain of California rainbows was planted in Michigan. Seth Green then shipped eggs to Colorado and Wyoming and also established the rainbow in Patagonia.

Both planned introductions and basic backyard, bucket biology are responsible for the spread of brown trout. In 1880, Fred Mather received a shipment of brown trout eggs, hatched them, and planted them with little fanfare and fewer accurate records. The following year, eggs arrived from both Loch Leven, Scotland, and from the chalkstreams of Hampshire, and were planted in Michigan.

Brown trout were considerably more controversial than rainbows. Then as now, they were apt to be overall more selective, less active during the middle of the day, and generally difficult to catch. But they also survived splendidly in the less-than-pristine waters that Americans were fishing as populations grew and water quality diminished.

Increasingly, at the turn of the century it was to the transplanted rainbows and browns that American anglers were casting their flies. The flies they were casting were wet flies, of the sort labeled by historians as "fancy flies" — the beautiful and exotic creations that in our modern parlance can only be termed attractor flies. Parmachene Belle, Scarlet Ibis, Durham Ranger, Ibis and White, Butcher, Wickham's Fancy — these are the wet flies that were dressed heavily and, to our modern way of thinking, were fished more like lures than flies. The reliance on flash and attraction rather than imitation certainly puts them in the lure category, when you try to analyze why trout eat the more garish of the patterns. More often than not, these flies were fished in multiples, with sometimes up to four droppers and a stretcher, or end fly. Gut was widely used as leader and tippet material, and oiled silk the preferred line.

Rods were, increasingly, split bamboo, whether from the shop of Leonard, the more affordable rods of Charles Orvis, or the widely distributed models available from Sears, Roebuck and Montgomery Ward.

All the casting gear was in order for the next big step, which was the introduction of the dry fly and imitation on American waters. The Catskills are where this took place, and Theodore Gordon is the angler who effected the development.

AMERICA'S COTTON

Understand from the onset: Gordon is a demigod. His effect on American angling — and later, the influence that has been credited him — are phenomenal. Like Gingrich says, Gordon was our Charles Cotton.

If Theodore Gordon hadn't lived, we would have found it necessary to invent him. In many ways, perhaps we have. "Though once a real person, he has become our myth," says John McDonald.

Gordon was regularly coughing up blood at the end of his life, and he was assumed to have died from tuberculosis. But it has been recorded that Gordon was a heavy smoker, rolling his own, one-handed, sucking lustily for several puffs, then tossing the cig away, only to begin rolling the next. TB sounds pretty romantic, especially if you call it consumption, but fact is, our main man may well have smoked himself to an early death. Given his long history of frailty, it's no surprise tobacco carried him away.

But back to the myth. He was as well unlucky in love. A couple of oft-cited photos exist of Gordon and a woman, but nobody seemed to know who she was.

It's easy enough to find frailty and human failing. Heroes are easy to destroy and hard to find. And Gordon is certainly well suited to be one of our angling heroes. He was an excellent, thoughtful writer, and our modern, distinctly American form of angling has a direct lineage back to him. He was a wonderfully complete representative of angling at that time, and the fact that angling came to be distinctly our tradition makes Gordon an essential figure in the history of our sport. As Schullery stated, the biggest problem in understanding Gordon is keeping him in context.[37]

Here's his story, nutshelled:

Theodore Gordon was born in Pittsburgh in 1854, son of prosperous parents. His father died a year later, and Gordon bounced around with his mother between Pennsylvania, Savannah, and New Jersey. He probably fished extensively during his early years. His health was frail, and his mother took great pains to keep him in a climate that best suited his health.

He is known to have worked in finance — brokerage, accounting, and securities. By 1900 he was tying flies professionally and traveling between homes in New York and the rivers of the Catskills.

As early as 1890 he was writing for the British journal *The Fishing Gazette,* where he became a familiar contributor, and as John McDonald has pointed out, where he published his most sophisticated essays. The material printed under his name in *Forest and Stream,* in which he began writing in 1903, was written for a more general audience.[38]

Gordon called these essays "little talks," and if you read them all together, as they are presented in *The Complete Fly Fisherman,* they represent a fairly astounding body of work. Bear in mind, though, that they were written over a period of 25 years, and many of these pieces included are personal: letters which no one ever read, except the addressee, until John McDonald assembled them in a cohesive presentation.

Gordon's passbooks into history were Norris' *American Angler's Book,* Ronalds' *Fly-Fisher's Entomology,* and most important, Halford's *Floating Flies and How to Dress Them*. In 1890, Gordon wrote to Halford, and in a part of their correspondence, Halford sent him a set of chalkstream dry flies.

Fascinating stuff, for sure, but what exactly did Gordon do? He personified the Catskill school of fly dressing, delicate, sparsely tied flies; he for all practical purposes popularized the American dry-fly tradition; he combined a strict theory of imitation with a generalized approach. His own Quill Gordon he adapted in shade and coloration to serve any number of imitative purposes.

Gordon fished everything at his command — nymphs (he corresponded with Skues as well), wet flies, and dry flies, never lapsing into the purist approach. The Neversink was his home water, but he fished throughout the Catskills. He fished in America and his best writing went to England. He was in constant contact with the British anglers, while creating a distinctive American style of fishing.

Gordon was, in short, an innovator of nothing in particular and a popularizer of everything; a great fishing writer and a solid link with the British tradition in an American setting. He combined the brilliance of the best British angling minds with the unfettered opportunity still to be found on American waters.

"He performed the joint services of a Halford and a Skues,"[39] according to John McDonald, and he did it in a country rich with freestone rivers and limestone creeks and a burgeoning number of enthusiastic anglers who could care less about the rules for proper fishing. The emerging American angler consumed the wisdom of the centuries, and without batting an eye, applied the wisdom contained therein to the catching of fish in an exuberant new country full of rushing rivers and increasing leisure time to spend on them.

Gordon assembled the palette of the historical development of fly fishing and with a broad brush painted this accumulation of experience and wisdom across the clean canvas that was the rivers of America.

He was a bridge, and, above all else, a fisherman, and that's perhaps why his appeal and his influence are so hard to define. He died in 1915 and is buried in New York City. There's much to be learned from his writing, which John McDonald collected in *The Complete Fly Fisherman*. Have at it.

After Gordon, George LaBranche would close the circle, proclaiming once and for all that you could use any fly you chose, and — horror of horrors — you could fish the water and not the rise. Surely a neolithic approach.

This bit of independence, however, opened the door for a steady stream of anglers and writers unfettered by tradition or propriety. The only thing that mattered now was results — not the method chosen to pursue them. Jennings would come along to do our entomology. Bergman and Leisenring would show us how to fish. Schwiebert and Brooks would lead to Swisher and Richards, and we would be delivered into the Age of Pretension and the birth of Bug Latin.

CHAPTER SEVEN

THE BIRTH OF BUG LATIN AND THE AGE OF PRETENSION

With Theodore Gordon's death opened the era of distinct and well-defined American tradition. Once an upstream approach and both floating and sinking flies were accepted as tools in the angler's arsenal, serious fishing progress ensued. The time between Gordon's death and World War II was a rich one, and the standards and traditions of angling in the eastern U.S. often were born and matured in the same decade.

World War II would bring substantial changes to American angling. Synthetic materials would make spin fishing possible, and an exploding demand for recreation changed the face of American angling. Eventually fly fishing would emerge from its dark ages, and when it did, the arena would once again expand tremendously, growing beyond the boundaries of a few sheltered, timbered valleys in New York and Pennsylvania.

Within a year of Theodore Gordon's death, George La-Branche published *The Dry Fly and Fast Water,* and opened the next chapter in the development of American fly-fishing traditions.

Again, the publication of a book usually signals not the first appearance of a particular practice or technique, but the recognition that this technique was established, its efficacy proven through time and trial. This is where LaBranche fits in, and the thing he introduced to the literature was as much a landmark as the other four established by John Waller Hills' approach to the history of fly fishing.

For after imitation, casting to a particular fish, casting upstream, and all of the above with a floating fly — which were Hills' four landmarks — LaBranche presented the next landmark, and acknowledged it was that anglers were well within bounds of propriety to fish not only to specific rising fish, but to water where fish might be. LaBranche made it cool to fish the water, with whatever kind of fly you wanted to fish.

LaBranche's home water was the Brodheads, and this stream played an important role in the thought that went into *The Dry Fly and Fast Water,* though his work was modelled on his fishing of a variety of Catskills streams. The tight small waters that made often impossible technical demands on the caster and angler were where LaBranche excelled. His skills at casting and line manipulation were well known and acknowledged, and he was regarded as one of the finest anglers of his day.

The Fishing Gazette, Britain's oldest fishing weekly, reported an exhibition during one of his visits.

> *This remarkable caster cast the dry fly in places in which it would be extremely difficult to drop a worm, under overhanging alders and blackberry bushes, around trunks of trees, casting at will on to particular leaves that the fly might drop thence like a caterpillar from an oak leaf. His fishing is smooth and entirely effortless . . . his flies go where he wishes them to go and act as he directs them when they get there.*[40]

His particular skills at casting and placing the fly, and at manipulating it and fishing it once it was on the water, gave natural rise to his theory of presentation as a permutation of the theory of imitation.

According to LaBranche, the most important consideration in imitating a natural insect was imitating the ways it acted, rather than the way it looked. The position of the fly upon the water was the most important consideration, followed by its action, its size, its form, and lastly, the color of the fly.

Imitation here takes on a new aspect — anatomical imitation takes second place to behavioral imitation. The way the fly is presented becomes an element of imitation, one of paramount importance. This approach can be seen to have risen naturally out of the geography of American trout streams.

Tumbling mountain rivers of the United States demanded this approach. The slick pools and runs that gave rise to the British tradition tailored a style of fishing suited to that water. Once Gordon had taken these technical developments and adapted them to American waters, the natural next step was the one that LaBranche took, making all of this applicable to American waters.

American rivers were still under a kind of exploration. They hadn't had all the information gleaned from them that they would in the next few decades, and in figuring out just what made them work, a new approach was inevitable.

Hundreds of years went into the British tradition, and once the streams were civilized and managed, codification ensued, requiring rules and the inflated atmosphere of purism and propriety that was personified in Halford. "It is the unwritten law of the dry-fly man on a chalk-stream to eschew any but the legitimate method," Halford wrote in 1913.[41]

This kind of narrow, rule-ridden approach comes after thorough familiarity with a particular fishery, artificial rules designed to preserve the purity of the sport. The same thing would happen in the U.S. in later decades, to a lesser degree than in England, but in the early twentieth century, investigation was still under way, and LaBranche made a substantial contribution to recognizing a distinctive American approach to stream fishing.

LaBranche's best-known technique, if his work must be boiled down to a single technique, was his invention of the artificial hatch, wherein the dry fly was repeatedly cast to a promising piece of water, in essence creating its own hatch. The theory was that, after seeing a fly pass overhead time and time again, the trout would begin to suspect a hatch was in progress and eventually rise to the artificial. The Pink Lady, a fly LaBranche developed, was his favorite pattern, and he was often known to go through a season fishing nothing else, so successful was he at imitating the behavior of natural insects. His pattern needs were served well with this most general of attractors because he imitated insect behavior precisely.

The same theory of generalized appearance and behavioral imitation emerged in the fishing of Edward Ringwood Hewitt. He developed the dry-fly spiders, the skaters and bivisibles, his own series of loosely representative fly patterns that relied on behavior and manipulation on the surface to move trout. Skating spiders were one of Hewitt's more interesting developments. The fly is simple: two hackles, concave sides facing each other, tied on a #16 dry-fly hook. The fly is designed to be skated across the surface, raising fish unwilling to rise otherwise. Charles Fox wrote about the skating spider in the early 60s, as did Joe Brooks in the 70s. Part of the magic and lore of the spiders is the quality of hackle required to tie them; only the stiffest, longest fibered hackles can be used. In this day of genetic hackle, it's not such a big deal, but when they were invented, getting the materials represented a substantial challenge.

What still remained to be developed was a distinctly American entomology. What is required for this task is someone with the angling knowledge and experience combined with a willingness to indulge in a precise scientific approach to insect identification.

Louis Rhead had made a cursory pass at pairing artificial flies with natural insects on American waters, but he fell short. He used names of his own invention to describe much of what he observed, making it unusable and confusing. He not only failed to move the process along but actually held it back for a while. Part of the reason for this was no doubt commercially inspired. Rhead manufactured a line of artificials called Nature Flies, about which he wrote in his books and had a vested interest in controlling the names of the artificial, much as he controlled their manufacture. It would be almost 20 years before the next logical step was made. When it was, Preston Jennings made it.

In 1935 Jennings published *A Book of Trout Flies* which represented the first serious and viable approach to an American aquatic insect entomology. To put his accomplishment into proper perspective, Jennings did for American fishing what Ronalds had done a hundred years earlier for the British. He made the connection between an artificial fly and a scientifically identifiable genus and species of insect. At the same time, Jennings' catalogue of flies sorted through a hundred years of fly patterns — much as Bowlker had done in 1747 with the British accumulation — eliminating everything that was non-imitative, though the Royal Coachman was retained, simply because it was so popular and so successful.

It's almost as if he felt he had to justify the inclusion on imitative grounds, so he wrote "There IS a Royal Coachman," published in *Esquire* magazine in July 1956, in which he describes the nymphal form of the dry fly and identifies it as *Isonychia bicolor.*

Perhaps the most popular book on fishing written so far appeared in 1938 when the fishing editor for *Outdoor Life,* Ray Bergman, published *Trout.* Bergman has been called the

Dr. Spock to a whole generation of fishermen.[42] *Trout* was considered for years the one book to have on your shelves if you are only having one.

Bergman's low-key, homespun approach to as complex a subject as fly fishing for trout is irresistible, and once you've gotten into Bergman it stays with you always. As Schwiebert has described it, "*Trout* has a warmly personal narrative quality that has enabled it to dominate the field long after its technical recommendations and tackle were rendered obsolete by new methods and materials."[43]

The same is true today, and like no other book, *Trout* is about fishing. There is tackle, there is fly information, and there is a lot of other stuff that is a product of its time. But there is also a lot about fishing itself, that elusive thing that gets tied up in the literature and the innovation and becomes difficult to separate from a lot of other things. This is Bergman's timeless appeal. He wrote about fishing.

On the eve of the United States' entry into World War II, James Leisenring, a machinist from Allentown, Pennsylvania, produced *The Art of Tying the Wet Fly*. Due to the political concerns of the time, the work went relatively unnoticed. Leisenring was to the rebirth of wet-fly fishing what Theodore Gordon was to dry-fly fishing. A stubborn infatuation with the dry fly prevented a full appreciation of Leisenring's work, and this is still the case today. Even after Vernon Hidy added his *Fishing the Flymph* to the revised edition, it remains a relatively obscure method and approach. The flymph is still obscure, but this intermediate stage, between the nymph and the fly, is a killing approach, though it is little practiced and little known. Straight nymph fishing has had a better revival than the traditional, and effective, wet-fly techniques that Leisenring and Hidy expounded.

Schwiebert wrote about Leisenring in his introduction to the combined edition of the two books:

American anglers have largely forgotten James Leisenring in following the more glamorous heroes of American fly-fishing, but it was Leisenring who quietly adapted the wet-fly tactics of Stewart and Skues to the fly hatches of American waters, just as Gordon and LaBranche transplanted British dry-fly methods to the swift-rivers of the Catskills.[44]

Following World War II, America plunged itself whole-heartedly into recreation. Outdoors was in, and fishing was a big part of it, though not necessarily fly fishing. Technological developments that came out of World War II brought a wealth of new materials for fabricating fishing tackle, and the impact these new materials would have on angling was unprecedented. Nylon was one of these new materials, and so was fiberglass, and suddenly spin-fishing was all the rage. Fiberglass revolutionized rodmaking, and the technology suddenly drove the tackle business, and the tackle business took control of how Americans fished.

The decades that followed have been called the Dark Ages of Fly Fishing. Not a few fine anglers and writers fell under the spell of spin-fishing, and entranced with the technology, fell head over heels into the new method. Strangely, once identified with spin-fishing, many writers never were able to earn back their credibility among the devoted fly fishers. But many bridged the gap between the two styles with good taste, and foremost among these had to have been Al McClane.

Al McClane went to work for *Field & Stream* in 1947, taking over as fishing editor when Ted Trueblood went back to Idaho. Shortly thereafter, as Reiger explains in *Fishing with McClane,* McClane led the way around the world. The airline boom of the 1950s made fishing an international sport for just about everyone. McClane at once pioneered much of it, served as the reporter, the tutor, the master angler, and the guide. Through the 50s, 60s, and 70s, McClane was a household word among anglers, both fly fishermen and others, and a lot of today's anglers grew up reading the inspiring essays of McClane.

These years may well have been the Dark Ages of Fly Fishing, but the things that were published during these decades were for the most part of high quality. The Dark Ages of Fly Fishing were not dark ages of fly-fishing thought.

Art Flick's *Streamside Guide to Naturals and Their Imitations* was published in 1947, offering a simplified approach to imitations of the typical hatches of the Catskills. It was a book as significant as Ronalds', and even more so in 1969, when the revised edition was published and the illustrations clearly showed artificial flies next to natural insects in perfect, clear, color photographs. It was a mind-snapper for a generation of anglers. This was the book that pulled it all together.

Vincent Marinaro's *Modern Dry-Fly Code* contributed to the knowledge of fishing hard-fished streams and increasingly more selective trout.

In 1955 Ernest Schwiebert wrote *Matching the Hatch* when he was a sophomore in college. His erudition belied his youth, but his credentials were impeccable and his experience broader already than anglers decades his superior. In *This Wonderful World of Trout* Charles Fox explains how Schwiebert was groomed for his role in American fly fishing. When Ernest was barely a teenager, his father put him in the hands of Bill Blades to teach him to tie flies. Later he was turned over to Frank Steel, the champion tournament caster, to learn to handle the equipment. Formal training in architecture and fine art provided the opportunity to develop the discipline and the skills required of a modern angling master, entomologist, and illustrator.

Schwiebert explained in the introduction to his next book, *Nymphs,* how his publisher predicted *Matching the Hatch* would last 20 years. Indeed it did, but by modern standards the illustrations were silly — small, difficult-to-use pictures of similar-appearing mayflies. As an initial step in developing an American aquatic entomology, it certainly did what it intended. But more important, it coined a phrase with its title. *Nymphs,* which was published in 1973, provided more information and more fly patterns than most anglers will ever get around to tying.

Schwiebert's approach was a healthy step away from the narrow regionalism that had begun to dominate entomological studies, and it set the pattern for those who would follow later, with their own contributions.

Regionalism was a constant problem. Angling writers and researchers had blinders on when it came to seeing anything other than the waters right in front of their eyes. It would be almost 30 years before any real inroads were made to the entomology of the Rocky Mountains and the western states.

By the time Schwiebert did his follow-up volume, his style and execution had developed considerably.

Joe Brooks introduced Doug Swisher and Carl Richards to the world in 1970. These two amateur researchers from Michigan set yet another new standard in American entomology with the publication of *Selective Trout* in 1971.

The no-hackle fly designs Swisher and Richards pioneered were a big departure from the hackled designs that predominated through the 1960s. Their theory of fly design and construction, and especially their considerable photographic skills in portraying the finding of their work, were all new. And so were a lot of the insect hatches they described. Of particular interest is their work on emergers and the nymphal stages of hatching insects.

With *Matching the Hatch* already enshrined as a classic, *Nymphs* coming on its heels 19 years later, and the emergence of Swisher and Richards, another tradition was born in American fly fishing — Bug Latin. No longer were distance casting and creeled trout the only competitive aspects of fly fishing — taxonomy reared its ugly side, and the angler not well versed in Latin names of insects had to be pretty careful around a lot of tackle shops.

Anyone who witnessed one of these early confrontations couldn't help but be a little bit scared at first and disgusted later. It was like a showdown, each angler springing the name of an insect encountered recently on the other, a give-and-take of one-upmanship that only stalled out when one or the other ran out of bug names — or when another angler strolled up to bandy about a bit of the Latin and try to back another down with a blast of taxonomy.

The stage was set. Bug Latin was firmly established as coin of the realm in the vanguard of the sport. There's no doubt that the increased knowledge and codification had value, but much of it was important in only a very limited situation. And much of it is not new at all, rather a rehash of things done in the past, fallen out of fashion and then given a new wrap of hackle and a reintroduction.

IN OVER OUR HEADS

Alfred Ronalds could have done the same thing in his book, but he had too much class to speak a language anglers didn't want to learn. He stuck to common, fisherman's lingo, and he's become a classic.

But this was not to be the case with the modern angler-entomologists. Bug Latin took hold. Though LaFontaine, Caucci and Nastasi, and Arbona all made substantial contributions to the entomology and fly-making traditions, the whole thing somehow lost something of the fun associated with the sport, once taxonomy was the issue rather than fishing. The intellectual stakes became both too competitive and a bit too technical. Fly patterns were designed that approximated very specialized behaviors of insects, fish were caught on them, then the patterns foisted on the reading public. Fly patterns began to sport the remnant nymphal shuck, the insect at the stage after emergence from the nymph stage, after the emerger stage, but just before the floating adult.

Of course, what had happened is that Swisher and Richards had upped the ante, and once their photography was published, everyone got in on the act. Observation and study took giant steps, and the art of imitating natural insects was suddenly predicated on a freeze-frame view of the aquatic insect through the entire cycle of its life.

General, non-imitative fly patterns were out of the question. The Age of Pretension was hard upon us, and Bug Latin was the Language of State.

Right now we seem to be in a real period of simplification — at least there's a spate of books out designed to demystify the sport and make it accessible.

At this point in this narrative it becomes tough to talk about history. Like John Waller Hills trying to get a fix on Skues even as he was under Halford's spell, it's time to shut up. We've come to the end of our dead guys, and only a fool forges a history from his own thoughts.

This pretty much brings us up to date, insofar as anyone who learns to fish these days will be drawing off the past 50 or 60 years, in which is included the prior 400 years.

Up to and including most of the 1970s, anyone learning to fish in the United States relied on the tradition we've reviewed. Their hatches were the hatches of the Catskills for the most part. In the 70s a remarkable change came about — the West, regarded for its wild and rugged rivers, suddenly began to get the attention the fishing deserved, and no longer would the Eastern Establishment hold sway over the national fly-fishing consciousness. Once regarded as crude, homespun, and provincial — and perhaps rightly so — a new breed of angler came on the scene as national demographics began to shift and increasing numbers of young people moved west for the quality of life it offered. The West began to take its place in the national angling picture.

Strangely, the West began to come into its own just as the first outbreaks of Bug Latin were sweeping the East and Midwest. Perhaps the unsullied rivers of the Rocky Mountains offered relief from the high pretension that had come to dominate the sport, the physical freedom of the landscape offering a similar freedom from intellectual demands, as the atmosphere of the sport had begun to rival the British in its inflated sense of propriety and exactness. The West was a good safety valve for this growing pressure.

The fishing was also a hell of a lot better than it was in the East, and the word spread quickly once it got out.

CHAPTER EIGHT

THE WEST
COMES OF AGE

The 1970s marked a turning point in the national fishing consciousness regarding important centers of angling. A large shift of the population to the mountain west and the mountain states had a lot to do with this.

Western waters and trout had always been somewhat of an exotic deviation for the serious angling done in the East. Rivers in the West were big and windy, trout were not known to be particularly selective, and angling techniques were held to be primitive at best.

Certainly enough anglers had traveled west to fish: Leisenring spent time in Yellowstone Park, employed to keep trout on the menus in the restaurants — but he returned to the Brodheads to do his serious research and development. Joe Brooks was a regular at Dan Bailey's in Livingston and almost a fixture on the Yellowstone River.

Fishing in the West — and here the West means the Rocky Mountains — was always more a part of day-to-day life and less a recreational specialty than it ever was in the eastern United States. The quality of fishing also surpassed that of eastern fishing. The western tradition, although far less developed and less sophisticated in terms of exact imitation and technical formality, had its own history and formalism, however inexact by eastern standards.

The size of the rivers, the size and naiveté of the fish, and the raw nature of the uncivilized West all contributed to the development of a far different tradition from what developed in the East.

Here's roughly how it came about.

Western trout fishing was something that came naturally with the frontier, exploration, and settlement.

As mentioned earlier, white men fished the West as soon as they came into the country, as early as 1803, when the Lewis and Clark expedition headed towards the Pacific, but it was not necessarily fly fishing.

Rainbow trout and steelhead were native only to the Pacific Coast — though there is some speculation that rainbows may have ascended the Snake River and slipped up Pacific Creek and across the Continental Divide through the swamp at Two Ocean Plateau during an especially high water year, and descended Atlantic Creek into the headwaters of the Missouri drainage. It seems to be a theory that is out of fashion. Joe Brooks wrote it up. It's a wonderful thought. It could have happened, but if it didn't, it still makes a far better story.

Regardless of how the newcomers came, the trout of the intermountain West was the cutthroat until the latter quarter of the nineteenth century.

In 1836 Gairdner's salmon was identified in California.[45] *Salmo gairdneri* was the name worn by the rainbow trout for decades. In 1855, *Salmo irideus* was the name given the freshwater rainbow. It was an age of splitters in the taxonomic world, and nearly every drainage in the West had its own subspecies of trout for a while.

In 1878 — perhaps earlier — the first rainbows were shipped from California to Michigan, and from there they traveled to New York. Some records report 1874 and 1875 when rainbow eggs were sent from the Pacific slope to the Midwest.[46] From there it was nothing to stock them in streams where they didn't stock themselves by simply expanding their range where suitable habitat was found.

Eastern brook trout were introduced to California and the Rocky Mountain states in 1872. Brown trout introductions began shortly thereafter.[47]

In February, 1883, Fred Mather, who managed the hatchery at Cold Spring Harbor, Long Island, received a shipment of brown trout eggs from Baron Lucius von Behr, president of the German fishing society (Deutscher Fischerei Verein). Part of the shipment went to a sister hatchery at Caledonia, New York, and the rest went to Northville, Michigan, where the Pere Marquette became the first American river to be stocked with browns. In 1884, the Loch Leven strain came to the U.S. Brown trout were stocked in 38 states by the turn of the century, with Montana getting them in 1889, Wyoming in 1890, and Colorado in 1903.[48]

There was a pretty well-developed sport fishery going on with the native cutthroat populations already. The new imports only improved the fishing.

In Colorado the sporting tradition is well documented, and 130 years ago fishing was a fashionable pastime outside of Denver, on the South Platte at Deckers. This would have put it about 1860. Denver anglers could hit the South Platte via wagon road, and early records indicate it was well traveled. In 1874, the Denver South Park & Pacific Railroad opened the Platte Canyon, and the river was touted to residents and tourists alike, famed for the quality of its fishing and the fact that it was one of the few rivers on the front range that hadn't been polluted by mining effluent.

An unusual development took place early in the century on the South Platte — the establishment of private water.

By 1921 the private water of the Wigwam Club had been sealed off to the public by the upper crust of Denver's angling society. Special rules and regulations, as well as vigorous stocking from the club's hatchery, provided an early model for quality fishing and some outstanding angling, even if the concept were in direct contrast to the western democratic tradition.

While the concept of private waters was long established in the East, and of course in Britain, it was an unusual approach for the West, standing squarely in opposition to the western mindset which reviled regulation of any sort and treasured public access.

The similarities to the eastern aristocratic tradition didn't end there. One incident in particular stands out in sharp contrast to everything we think the West stands for. It took place at this same fishing locale.

John Monnett, in *Cutthroat and Campfire Tales,* relates an incident in which a Wigwam Club member, Cliff Welch, fished — and very successfully — a March Brown with a split-shot on the leader. The club officials came unglued and demanded Welch give up the practice or leave the club. Surely his thoughts must have been with G.E.M. Skues, if he was familiar with the same British intolerance. If not, his thoughts must have been as dark as Skues', who experienced the same sort of censure for fishing a nymph on an English chalkstream. Just because the West was new and unsettled didn't mean the East and Britain had a monopoly on intolerance and closed minds.[49]

Whether or not Welch quit fishing the weighted nymph or quit the Club is unknown, but as these things are apt to happen, the technique he used, however vile and unthinkable in the context in which it appeared, did catch fish, big fish, when no one else was catching anything at all. A tradition was born. Welch broke the code, and if you fish the South Platte today — or any number of rivers in Colorado — you'd better know how to fish a #18 or #20 or #22 nymph below a split-shot if you expect to do well.

Throughout the West, wherever people traveled, and they were traveling more and more through the nineteenth century, the fishing often caught their imaginations. A lot of the travel and tourism, and hence the fishing, in those days centered around what would become Yellowstone Park in 1872. The wonders of Yellowstone were regaled in the East, drawing a steady stream of tourists who could afford to make the trip. Fishing was part of their experience. They fished to the native cutthroats, and they did well.

In 1886, George Wingate published a travelogue, *Through the Yellowstone on Horseback,* and his activities included a good sampling of the fly fishing for native trout. What he found were fish of six and seven pounds at Tower Falls. Fishing Yellowstone Lake he averaged fish of two pounds. On a particular morning, "the catch was twenty-four, weighing 40 pounds, only one trout being under a pound, which under the circumstances, was as good fishing as could be desired."[50]

Three years after Wingate's tales of the Park were published, brook trout were stocked in the Firehole River and brown trout followed in 1890.[51] Over the next 10 years, travelers fished regularly and wrote of their experiences. It was during this time the classic Yellowstone fishing stunt became popular: Anglers discovered they could catch a trout from icy waters, then, without moving, cook it by swinging it into an adjacent thermal feature. Fishing Cone in Yellowstone Lake was the typical location for this stunt, though it was performed regularly on the Firehole River, too.

In the early 1900s the railroads reached the gates of the Park at Gardiner and West Yellowstone, and from then on out, the West was for all practical purposes open to fishing.

By the 1920s and 30s, Montana anglers were well along on their own tradition of fishing. This was especially evident in the fly tyers who thrived amidst what was for all purposes a cultural vacuum.

Norman Means devised the Bunyan Bug, which was little known to anglers outside Montana then and now until Norman Maclean wrote about it in *A River Runs Through It*. In the early 1970s it was still possible to find a few remaining Bunyan Bugs on faded counter-cards in small-town tackle shops — just as it was not uncommon to find troves of an even more important Montana original, Pott's Hair Flies.

Franz Pott was a wig maker who virtually invented the woven-hair fly in the 1920s. His techniques, for which he had two patents, utilized animal-hair hackles and woven segmented bodies. For years these flies were all it took to catch fish in Montana. The names of the patterns were Sandy Mite, Lady Mite, Mr. Mite — all derivative of the hellgrammite, which is the local term for the giant stonefly nymph. The natural stonefly nymphs were prime trout bait for years, easily gathered and irresistible to trout.

In the early 1930s Don Martinez set up shop in West Yellowstone. A Californian and a fly tyer, Martinez is credited with inventing the Wooly Worm, though what he did was popularize it in the Wyoming and Montana streams where it served as a fine imitation of the giant stonefly nymphs. Martinez is acknowledged as the first fly fisherman and the first angler with a thorough grounding in entomology to set up shop in the Yellowstone area.

At about the same time, Dan Bailey, also an Easterner, began fishing in Montana. Bailey was a veteran of the golden age of the Catskills tradition, and as such, his sophistication and knowledge were well beyond what was required to catch fish in the Rocky Mountains. The tradition and practice in Montana still appeared relatively primitive to the eastern consciousness. To anyone with common sense, however, this tradition hadn't yet been trampled and ruined.

By 1937 he'd moved his fly-tying business to Livingston. From these new headquarters, he set about not only introducing eastern imitative theory but developing a substantial number of western fly patterns as well.

Perhaps the most significant of these is the series of hairwing dry flies developed with Lee Wulff. Wulff didn't invent hair-wing dry flies, but he might as well have, so thoroughly were they identified with him.

Bailey typified the western approach to fly fishing — offering the fish something they could see and something that made them strike. The specific imitation of particular insects was a long way off. Bailey himself explained in a letter to Preston Jennings:

> *My idea of flies is quite different from yours, so I doubt that any of my contributions would suit you. My theory which is borne out in practice is that the trout's version is so different from the human's that there is little value in working from the naturals. As long as a dry floats well and comes fairly close to imitating a large group of insects it does the trick. Changes which I have made in flies have been based on the trout's acceptance. That being the case, my patterns might look less like the natural than English or Eastern flies.[52]*

Bailey created an empire based on impressionistic fly tying that is still going strong today.

At about the same time that Franz Pott and Dan Bailey were developing their tackle business, a fly tyer from Butte was looking to get into the game. George Grant became interested in fly tying in 1928. While he held a number of jobs which could well have led him elsewhere, he caught a whiff of truth in his business association with the movers and shakers in Butte during the heyday of mining, namely, that "success and contentment were not synonymous."

Grant says it better than anyone can in *The Master Fly Weaver.*

In retrospect, it now is apparent that I was simply pre-destined to lead an idyllic life wading fabulous western trout streams; dressing artificial creations to copy aquatic insects and deceive the large wild trout that lived within them; enjoy the mystique and the endless variety that is part of the sport called flyfishing, but which to many of us, is a passport to another world.

And a bit later in the text, Grant writes one of the most wondrous sentences in all of fly fishing, one so full of promise and opportunity there is scarcely an angler who can't relate to it.

"In 1933 a wonderful thing happened — I lost my job."

For three years during the Depression, Grant lived on the Big Hole in the summers and tied flies in Butte in the winter, during a time he calls the Golden Era of trout fishing in Montana.

This has become an honorable tradition in today's angling. How tired do we get of hearing about one guide or another with advanced degrees or other badges of success who pitches it all aside simply because he wants to go fishing? These days, when there is too much of everything and too many of every occupation, that sort of decision in one's life has almost become cliché.

"Trout Bum" has become a semi-respectable moniker, and especially now that western fly fishing in particular and fly fishing in general have become such an industry, it is not an unprofitable trade-off, either. I like to think that George Grant provided the model for that lifestyle.

Grant is best known for taking the techniques of Pott and improving upon them. He had a tough time carving out a niche. He chose to do it by making flies that lasted, known for their durability.

"In the 1930-40 period in Western Montana it was not difficult to tie a fly that would catch trout — it would have been more difficult to tie one that would not," Grant says in *The Master Fly Weaver.*[53]

To operate a successful business meant carving out a chunk of the market, and Grant found himself sandwiched between Franz Pott in Missoula and Dan Bailey in Livingston. He soon had a piece of the action.

The next couple of decades in western fishing history were nothing more than a slow build-up to the day when western trout fishing would be recognized for the quality angling it offered.

Sometime in the late 30s, 1937 or 1938, Pat Barnes put the first McKenzie river boat on the Madison, and an entire float-fishing industry was born, though it wouldn't mature for a couple of decades.

Pat Barnes was the first tackle-shop proprietor in West Yellowstone to continue the tradition established by Californian Don Martinez. Dan Bailey continued to thrive in Livingston on the Yellowstone. Virtually anyone who took a trip to the Yellowstone area to fish stopped in at Bailey's shop to pick up flies or tackle, or at least called in for the latest fishing information.

The Yellowstone area remained the focus of western fishing, with the Montana, Idaho, and Wyoming rivers all within a few hours' drive of each other.

In 1950, Bud Lilly bought Don Martinez's shop in West Yellowstone. At the time, imitative entomology was still obscure and little known. Lilly says he didn't fish with dry flies until after he took over Martinez's business. Pott's Hair Flies and Norman Means' Bunyan Bug were the order of the day for fishermen in Yellowstone.

Dan Bailey continued to develop, tie, sell, and popularize the big dry flies, with the Wulff series, developed in the 1930s for Atlantic salmon, leading the charge.

If you had to choose the men who did the most to popularize western trout fishing, you'd probably come down to Dan Bailey, whose mail-order and retail tackle business was a model in the industry, and a highly visible booster for western fly fishing, and Joe Brooks, the incredibly popular fishing editor for *Outdoor Life* who fished and wrote about Montana right up until his death in 1972.

Brooks had a no-nonsense, almost minimalist approach to describing and demystifying fishing, and to read his work on trout fishing is to see yourself there, alongside him, fishing and catching trout. Brooks has a way of making you feel that all you had to do was show up at Widow's Pool to catch big western brookies. This had a tremendous effect on many anglers — anglers who never would travel west to fish and anglers who did in increasing numbers. Once Brooks and Bailey had established a beachhead, Bud Lilly sent out invitations to the party.

In the early 70s, the West broke wide open. Plenty of things contributed to the phenomenon, but the biggest reason the rivers of the West became so popular was because the fishing was so much better than it was in the East. The fish were bigger and more numerous, and if there was a serious dearth of insect study and categorization, it really didn't matter. It wasn't necessary at all. If you wanted plenty of water to fish and plenty of big fish to catch, here they were. And if you wanted to play entomological games and fine-tune difficult fish, there were plenty of spring creeks that demanded all the skills you had. The appeal was just that simple. The fishing was better.

This was overall a time of discovery and innovation in fly fishing. Polly Rosborough published *Tying and Fishing the Fuzzy Nymphs* in 1965. Doug Swisher and Carl Richards' landmark work *Selective Trout* came out in 1971. There were new thought and new blood in the sport. A new generation of anglers was turning its attention to anyplace there were trout to be fished.

"Suddenly there were writers who had spent the sixties patiently studying insects and now they were ready to publish their results," Bud Lilly says in *A Trout's Best Friend*.[54]

Bud Lilly put out his first catalogue in 1969, and suddenly the West Yellowstone area was truly on the map. One of Lilly's contributions was to showcase a number of creative fly tyers. Charles Brooks, Dave Whitlock, Al Troth, and many others found a market for their flies as well as an outlet for their innovative ideas through Bud Lilly's Trout Shop in West Yellowstone.

Another of Lilly's contributions to the sport of fly fishing was his concept of the Total Experience. He was serious. The geography and the landscape were every bit as important as the trout, in Bud Lilly's opinion. He pulled no punches when he encouraged anglers to enjoy themselves along the splendors of western streams.

Few fishermen will talk about it, but if you are fishing with a wife, husband, boyfriend or girlfriend, an important item of equipment can be a blanket. Who knows, maybe some sunny afternoon the two of you will be fishing away, tuned in to the natural setting and the mating of the salmon flies will inspire you. The experience doesn't get much more total than that.[55]

One of the West's first regional thinkers and writers was Charles Brooks. With the notable exception of *Waters of the Yellowstone with Rod and Fly* by Howard Back, which was published in 1930, there were few fly-fishing books available devoted to the region until Brooks published *Larger Trout for the Western Fly Fisherman* in 1970.

Since then the course of the West has been a steady growth in the number of fly fishermen and in many cases the quality of the fish.

Western entomology has developed, and exact imitation is the rule of the day on many streams. Happily, on many streams, the experts have simply refined their patterns a bit, dropped down a size or two, and continue to catch fish without precise imitation. Still, Bug Latin is alive and well in the West, and an increasing level of pretension is creeping into the tackle shops and along the streambanks.

CHAPTER NINE

THINGS BESIDES TROUT

A historical overview of fly fishing like this must necessarily leave a lot out. In order to cover the necessary ground, it's effective to stick to trout fishing. This works. The traditions of trout fishing remain the backbone of the sport, no matter what the quarry. Salmon may be an exception. There was quite a bit of parallel development in salmon fishing, in Great Britain and Europe, though it was a decidedly upper-class sport.

The same tradition naturally and easily made the trip across the Atlantic to flourish in the northeastern U.S. and Canada while the fish lasted.

We'll not dwell on it — if salmon fishing and history of same are your cup of tea, have at them. It's an expensive sport, available to few, and the published materials are far scarcer even than rare trout-fishing books. There are some techniques that have made the jump from salmon fishing to trout fishing and even saltwater, but beyond a nod and a wink, we're going to give the illustrious history of fly fishing for salmon short shrift.

Instead, we'll look at a tradition that developed in this country and remains distinctly American, that of steelhead and salmon fishing on the Pacific Coast. It has remained a relatively accessible sport, blue-collar, if you will, as opposed to the carriage-trade-dominated Atlantic salmon fishing.

Also, once American anglers began to penetrate the mainland, as it is easy to imagine, they cast flies over whatever bass water they encountered.

A definable lore developed around bass with the invention of bass bugs and lures designed for the fly rod, first a spinoff of trout practice, and eventually a sport unto itself.

IN THE BEGINNING, SALT

It could be said that American fly fishing has its origins in saltwater. This doesn't mean saltwater fly fishing has a longer tradition than freshwater in the U.S., but the first colonists had greater access to saltwater, having sailed across it and landed on its shores, and it's natural that tidewaters were the first to be graced with a fly in the New World. But just because the first flies were cast in the salt doesn't mean a tradition or preference was represented. After all, it was salmon and trout tackle that were first cast on American soil.

Saltwater fly fishing has always been with us, but the past 60 years have seen more development, inquiry, and gradual codification of saltwater fly fishing as a separate and distinct tradition. Technology has had a lot to do with this — the saltwater environment is deadly to many tackle materials, and the age of synthetics has allowed a lot of development and improvement in tackle suited to a harsh and corrosive environment — and fish that generally put freshwater fish to shame in terms of strength and size.

In no other type of fly fishing has technology played such a critical role in defining the sport as it developed. In fact, it is even now in a steady and rapid state of development. Every season sees fly patterns, techniques, and discoveries. Indeed, even the sport itself is constantly rediscovered, as has happened over the past hundred years.

Around 1843, an early mention of saltwater fly fishing appears in a British journal, *Bell's Life of London,* wherein the writer says he has been casting a fly in saltwater and fresh for 40 years. Chances are it goes a lot farther back than this — it just hasn't been uncovered yet.

The first saltwater fly-fishing references in the U.S. report fishing for striped bass and shad. These may have been fished in the rivers during spawning runs, but it's probable if they were fished during the upstream runs, they were fished in the estuaries and river mouths as well.

In *Natural History of the Fishes of Massachusetts,* published in 1833, Jerome V.C. Smith talked about fishing sea-run brook trout, and mentioned striped bass, though a definite connection with fly fishing wasn't specified. Finally, in 1849, Frank Forester in *Frank Forester's Fish and Fishing* encouraged anglers to fly fish for striped bass, and even made fly recommendations, which were, naturally, large salmon patterns.

Robert B. Roosevelt, relative to the illustrious, presidential Roosevelts, wrote about fly fishing for striped bass in the 1860s.

Fly fishing for saltwater fish has an unbroken history in the Northeast, though the popular focus shifted south to the more exotic fish of the Florida peninsula as the sport swept its way southward.

By the 1870s, anglers were filing fly-fishing stories from the St. Johns River, Homosassa, Biscayne Bay, and Florida Bay. Dr. James Henshall wrote *Camping and Cruising in Florida,* describing a trip he took in 1878. He talked of the abundant fish and their willingness to take a fly. His landed species included jack crevalle, seatrout, redfish, bluefish, snook, ladyfish, black bass, and "tarpum."

All of these were caught on a 12-foot ash and lancewood rod, which Henshall found a bit light for the species he was catching. He fished with big flies, #4/0 and #6/0, without much regard for pattern. It didn't seem to matter much. Colorful feathers were abundant, and ibis, egret, and spoonbill feathers found their way into his streamer patterns.

Bass and salmon flies formed the core collection of saltwater flies for the most part. Mary Orvis Marbury described the first saltwater pattern to be recorded, the Cracker, tied by George Trowbridge, in her landmark *Favorite Flies and Their Histories.*[56]

A.W. and Julian Dimock reported success on just about everything that swims in Florida waters when they traveled to the West Coast of the peninsula in the 1890s. They talked of fishing in the moonlight at Sarasota Pass, catching jacks, channel bass (redfish), gar, tarpon and Spanish mackerel, seatrout and ladyfish and even sheepshead occasionally. "Most fish on the Florida coast will rise to a fly. I have taken from one to a dozen varieties at every pass between Cedar Keys and Cape Sable."[57]

As observed by Paul Schullery, "Saltwater fly fishing, like streamer fishing, is susceptible to frequent rediscovery. It appears to have been rediscovered regularly for about a century in North America."[58]

Here's a perfect illustration. Allen Corson, fishing editor for the *Miami Herald*, got excited in 1949. Writing to J. Edson Leonard, author of *Flies*, he erroneously reported, "Only an accident created today's fly rod market. It was found, in June of 1947, that salt-water fish would take a fly. That is, the masses of anglers could do well, on a species no less respected than albula vulpes, the bonefish."[59]

Corson was writing about Joe Brooks' landing of a couple bonefish. Somehow Corson got it in his head that no one had caught a fly-rod fish in saltwater before Brooks nailed these bonefish. Corson's overall historical sense was perverted, for fly fishermen had been taking saltwater species for some time, and bonefish had been caught before Brooks caught his.

Holmes Allen of Miami caught a bonefish on a fly in Card Sound in 1924. He and fishing partners used to catch them with some regularity but, it appears, not on purpose.

Allen also caught a permit on fly tackle in 1928, near Boynton Beach, 50 miles north of Miami.

Homer Rhode landed permit and bonefish on fly tackle in 1930, according to George X. Sand.

Accidental bonefish catches were numerous — in fact, George LaBranche had witnessed one, but the prevailing attitude was that all such catches were incidental, if not accidental, and couldn't be duplicated on purpose.

Somebody finally did. In the summer of 1939, Capt. Bill Smith caught a bonefish at Little Basin off Islamorada, an eight-pound fish on a fly called Salt-us that he'd tied himself.

Smith had taken bonefish on a fly the year before — a fly decorated with a strip of pork rind. When he showed the fish and the fly to George LaBranche, who was staying in Islamorada at the time, LaBranche went ballistic, so ridiculing Smith for attaching bait to his fly that Smith slunk off, shamed but not deterred.

Smith dwelled on his near success for several months, and finally went out and did it again, on regulation tackle and an artificial fly without the addition of bait. The catch was witnessed and photographed for posterity.[60]

Smith was one of the first in a long line of illustrious guides in the Florida Keys.

Capt. Bill Smith's ex-wife, Bonnie Smith, was guide to George LaBranche. LaBranche hired Preston Pinder to instruct Bonnie how to fish bonefish. She taught fly casting to her sisters, Beulah and Frankee, and during World War II all three sisters were guides in the Keys. Bonnie served as guide for a soldier named Jimmie Albright, who landed his first bonefish on the trip. Albright later married Bonnie's sister, Frankee. Bill Smith taught Jimmie how to fish the flats. Bonnie, the first woman ever to land a permit on a fly, went on to guide Joe Brooks to his first fly-caught permit.[61]

Albright was an inspiration to a generation of guides. Following his lead, youngsters like Stu Apte learned the ropes and eventually made their own influential marks on saltwater fly fishing.

Along with bonefish, the tarpon is a critical glamour species in saltwater.

Tarpon were well known for their sporting qualities. Henshall had caught them up to 10 pounds on flies as early as 1878.

A.W. and Julian Dimock were perhaps the most well known of the early tarpon fishers. Conducting a couple of forays into Florida in the late 1800s, the Dimocks published *Florida Enchantments* in 1908, then A.W. followed it up in 1911 with *The Book of the Tarpon.*

In 1919 Fred Bradford Ellsworth wrote that tarpon had been taken on a fly for quite a long time and were being taken in the Panama Canal by this method.

William Mills of New York and Hardy's of England both offered tarpon streamers in their catalogues in the early 1900s.

In 1917 Bob McChristian moved to Florida and found already under way the design of the tarpon fly with the hackles set back towards the bend of the hook to prevent fouling on the false cast. This pattern was drawn from a New England bluefish fly first tied some 60 years before, placing the development of the Keys Tarpon Streamer at about 1857.

Giant tarpon continued to elude capture on fly tackle. The fish would eat the flies, but the tackle wasn't up to landing the giants.

George Bonbright landed one of the first giant tarpon ever on fly tackle. In a story published in *Field & Stream* in 1933, he describes the landing of a 136-pound fish on his own fly, the Bonbright Streamer. Speculation was that he attached a metal leader to his fly line, thus circumventing the inherent failure in gut leaders.

Regular catches of tarpon over a hundred pounds were not made until nylon leaders were developed after World War II and until fishing club rules were altered to allow a shock tippet. Before then, according to pioneer Florida light-tackle captain Jimmie Albright, the ceiling was about 50 pounds.

Rules in fishing are, of course, meaningless. But club rules dictated practice when club members were the only anglers really fishing light tackle for big fish.

According to Albright, in about 1953, Cliff Fitzgerald, Jr., caught a 115-pound tarpon on a 15-pound tippet. This was never acknowledged as an official catch, because the Rod and Reel Club recognized 12-pound tippets as the heaviest allowable. Not that the Rod and Reel Club had any legal right to determine what was and what was not a fair catch, but the club was the setting for almost all of the light-tackle and fly fishing done in Florida at the time.[62]

In 1955, fly-fishing rules established at the Rod and Reel Club finally allowed the use of shock tippet. That year, Charles Clowe, fishing Nine-Mile Bank with Cecil Keith, cast to, hooked, and landed a tarpon that weighed in at 101 pounds.

The growth of tarpon-fishing popularity had a lot to do with the attention Joe Brooks gave the fish. Brooks had the media exposure, and he fished with Capt. Stu Apte, no stranger to effective public relations, whose attention to detail and dedication to the hard work required to whip big fish were unsurpassed. Between the two they made a tremendous publicity machine for fly fishing for tarpon.

Popularization of saltwater fly fishing came with two accompanists: the increasing affordability of air travel, allowing more and more anglers to fish formerly prohibitively exotic destinations like Florida; and publicity and exposure in the popular press of the availability of saltwater fly fishing. Lefty

Kreh took advantage of the former in order to provide the latter. Lefty was a tremendous catalyst in popularizing saltwater fly fishing, and this popularization went hand in hand with the innovative casting methods he developed. These methods, while benefiting casting in general, had a profound effect on anglers' willingness to tackle saltwater, where they had been led to believe they must be able to cast long and powerfully. Though this was not necessarily the case, Lefty gave them the tools, and thus the confidence, to expand their range into the salt.

Lefty codified the saltwater fly-fishing experience in 1974 with the publication of *Fly Fishing in Salt Water.* This became a virtual Bible for an emerging generation of saltwater anglers. It was — and remains — indispensable reading.

Again, in 1988, Lefty published a landmark volume: *Salt Water Fly Patterns.* Not since the 70s, when Kenneth Bay published the skeletal but seminal *Salt Water Fly Tying,* had anyone catalogued saltwater fly patterns. Lefty hit them all and opened the gates for a flood of specialized pattern books, some of which may prove valuable and many of which may prove but minor pains in the growth of the sport.

BLUEWATER

The last great frontier in saltwater was bluewater fly casting for billfish. The dream of taking a billfish on fly tackle germinated in Florida waters, aided and nurtured by Florida captains, anglers, and expertise.

Dr. Webster (Doc) Robinson of Key West developed the system for taking billfish on the fly. Robinson was the angler, and his captain, Lefty Reagan, was on hand every step of the way, as was J. Lee Cuddy of Miami, whose input allowed Robinson to finally systemize billfishing technique.

Again, the Rod and Reel Club had a great deal to do with the configuration of tackle. Robinson used a 12-pound tippet because that was the maximum allowed by his club. A tarpon-sized rod, nine feet, for an 11 or 12-weight floating line and a popping bug rounded out the gear.

Robinson and Reagan worked out a system of teasing up the fish, then substituting the cast fly for the teaser once the boat was taken out of gear, presenting the fish a cast rather than a trolled fly in neutral. In 1962, on the Pacific side of Panama, Robinson cast to, hooked, and landed a 74 1/2-pound sailfish, the first billfish ever to fall to regulation fly casting.[63]

Robinson went on to capture the first marlin ever landed on a fly — a 145-pound striped marlin. Using Robinson's method, anglers began emulating his feats. J. Lee Cuddy followed on his heels, and it wasn't long before Billy Pate became the first angler to land five different billfish species on fly. The system developed by Robinson is still the way it's done offshore.

Developments in lines and rod design continue to open up the saltwater world to the fly rod. Wahoo and tuna have both become regular targets for serious fly rodders, in the Atlantic and off the West Coast, where long-range boats out of San Diego have begun plying Mexican waters. Long productive on conventional tackle, these waters are beginning to be explored by serious bluewater fly casters. There are still worlds to conquer for the fly rodder in the salt.

STEELHEAD: AMERICA'S OWN ANADROMOUS FISHES

In 1833 steelhead were still thought to be salmon and had not yet been identified as anadromous rainbow trout. By 1836, this oversight was rectified in *Fauna Borelai Americana* by Sir

John Richardson, when he named the fish after the naturalist Gairdner, Gairdner's salmon, *Salmo gairdneri.*

By the turn of the century, the seasonal runs of the salmon and steelhead were beginning to be understood. Steelhead and trout readily hit flies. Salmon were not as easy to fool. Thus the fly-fishing tradition for steelhead came into being, with San Francisco as the intellectual center.

Though the runs were known and anticipated — Paper Mill Creek, San Leandro River, and San Mateo Creek were most notable — it would be many decades before the entire spectrum of West Coast fishing would open up — and when it did, it would be almost too late for those fish.

The timber barons were the first to discover the tremendous steelhead runs. The English and eastern traditions found their first expressions on the Eel, deep in the virgin redwood country of Northern California. The Eel River would be regarded as the ultimate trophy fishery for fall and winter steelhead on fly.[64]

Dyerville on the Eel, and later Scotia, were the angling destinations. It was to Scotia that John S. Benn retired and set up shop as the Eel's first fly tyer.

Benn was born in County Cork, Ireland, immigrated to America in 1938, and set up shop in San Francisco. Benn's Coachman was one of the first fly patterns tied especially for steelhead fishing on that river. A lot of known patterns were adapted by Benn to steelheading and often named after Eureka's leading citizens.

The Rogue at this time was also becoming a well-known steelhead river. While the Eel was a river to visit, the more secluded Rogue became a river that drew settlers to its deep seclusion. The runs were smaller than the Eel, and the fish were smaller, too, but they went wild for the angler's flies. There developed on the Rogue a tradition of smaller, more somber patterns, often tied on double hooks.

Perhaps the Rogue's most celebrated visitor was Zane Grey, who purchased a cabin at Winkle Bar.

The Umpqua's North Fork, a national forest river with few private holdings along its banks, was the next great river to be recognized, in the 1920s, developing its own traditions of fly fishing and tackle recognized as suitable on the river. By this time, the 1930s, a seasonal migration of anglers was visited on the Eel, Rogue, and North Umpqua.

Meanwhile, Washington anglers were exploring their own water — the Stillaguamish and Skagit were believed to be on a par with the California streams. In 1942, North Fork Stillaguamish was set aside as fly-only fishing water.

Further development of steelhead fishing grew out of a well-developed tradition of tournament casting.

It's significant that steelhead fishing and tournament casting developed hand in hand on the West Coast. Big fish and big rivers demanded big techniques. Specialized tactics and specialized equipment, designed and developed to meet the demands of steelheading, were developed by the West Coast casting club members and other West Coast steelheaders.

Perhaps the most significant of these techniques was the double haul. Marvin Hedge, tournament caster, learned the double haul from Mooch Abrams, a Portland angler. It is said Abrams invented the double haul because of a physical impairment. It has since become part of every angler's arsenal.

Along with casting innovations, what developed in steelhead country was a tremendous number of variations on fly patterns. Standard fly patterns have been developed on every river for which there is a steelhead run.

Greased-line techniques, explained in 1935 in the famous volume *Greased Line Fishing for Salmon (and Steelhead)* by Jock Scott, found a ready audience on steelhead rivers. Donald Rudd, under the pen name Jock Scott, wrote of A.H.E. Wood's method for fishing salmon. The traditional method called for the fly to swing through, with the sunken silk line bellied, with the take coming at the bottom of the swing. Wood greased the line with animal fat, mended it, and kept the fly under tension without the belly. The greased-line technique found a home on winter runs of steelhead that required a deep fly, a long drift, and an accurate placement.

Harry Lemire, working with Syd Glasso and Ken McLeod, developed complicated combinations of shooting heads and running lines. For the most part, the well-known names of steelheaders are seldom known far from their home waters. It's a sport of specialized techniques tailored to individual streams and often single runs in individual rivers.

While Atlantic salmon and steelhead have many of the same characteristics, steelheading is a decidedly more democratic pursuit. The big names are seldom writers — Enos Bradner and Roderick Haig-Brown the exceptions — but instead are, first and foremost, fishermen, and perhaps fly tyers, too. Bradner was well known because he wrote for the *Seattle Times*. Ted Trueblood was the angling editor for *Field & Stream* before McClane. Most of the other big names in steelheading were fishermen — Harry Lemire, Ralph Wahl, Bill Schaadt, Syd Glasso, Brig. Gen. Noel Money.

The salmon and steelhead runs of the West Coast are mostly history now, compared to what they were even 25 years ago. Read *The Angler's Coast,* Russell Chatham's book of West Coast fishing stories. It's heady stuff — it mostly took place in the 60s and 70s and a lot of the great fishing is gone now.

Where steelhead are flourishing is in the Great Lakes runs. More than 60 rivers running into Lakes Huron, Michigan, and Superior support steelhead runs, and a dozen provide reliable angling for good runs of sizable fish.

These steelhead were planted in the 1870s, from Oregon stock. Lampreys, alewives, and ruthless gillnetting took them down to about nothing. The suitable rivers were restocked with coho and silver salmon to control burgeoning alewife populations in the lakes. Steelhead now hold in the lower reaches of the rivers in the fall, then in January and February move up into the spawning areas.

Doug Swisher and Carl Richards did a considerable amount of research into fishing these fish and published their findings in *Fly Fishing Strategy* in 1975. It's a specialized fishery, highly demanding, and one that has given rise to its own specialized techniques, tackle, and fly patterns.

BASS

By the 1840s Americans were already fly fishing warm waters for bass and bream. Fly fishing was well developed and functional long before bait casting and spinning, and it was natural that it once led as the premier method of bass fishing.[65]

All the time this was going on, of course, there was a running debate in the sporting press over whether or not the bass would take a fly at all. And, of course, once it had been determined that bass were susceptible to fly fishing, then the question arose as to which fish was more sporty, a bass or a trout.

The relative merits of the species were an argument early fomented as well. Because the origins of fly fishing were in trout, naturally the trout was at the top of the hierarchy. It was up to the bass to prove itself as worthy of pursuit as the trout.

Paul Schullery has tracked down an early bit of prejudice in an article appearing in an 1831 issue of *The American Turf Register*. The writer's comparison consisted primarily of the habitat, contrasting the "low, marshy lagoons' . . . turbid water, whose sluggish surface is not unfrequently rippled by the darting of the deadly mocassin," with the "verdant banks of some beautiful, rippling brook . . . gurgling and leaping in its living course to the ocean."[66]

Dave Whitlock sums up a similar perception, even in modern times: "Traditionalist fly fishers saw trout as a beautiful, delicate, highly intelligent, sophisticated fish living in pure, crystal-clear streams. They saw bass as coarse, dark, moody, gluttonous, and foolish, living in murky, stagnant swamps somewhere down South."[67]

Forest and Stream mentions bass fishing in St. Johns River in 1873, but it wasn't until the black bass' greatest champion James Henshall published *Book of the Black Bass* in 1881 that bass fever really got under way. American anglers went bass crazy in the 1880s and 90s.

Henshall is perhaps one of the most widely quoted American writers when it comes to bass — in fact, Arnold Gingrich said in *McClane's New Standard Fishing Encyclopedia* that Henshall is today one of the most quoted and least read of U.S. fishing writers. For better or for worse, whether you disagree or not, Henshall's infamous line regarding black bass was, "I consider him, inch for inch and pound for pound, the gamest fish that swims."

Bass-fishing history has more to do with the development of suitable artificials than it does with anything else. The flies and bugs typical of bass fishing are about the only things, save the environs where they are sought, that set off bass fishing as an endeavor separate from other types of fly fishing. This, however, is not insignificant.

At the time that anglers first began casting flies to bass, trout patterns were used. The favored artificial flies were big, and Henshall said the flies' patterns were not critical. In fact, the gaudier and more colorful the flies the better they were perceived to work. Most popular bass patterns were copies of trout flies. The fancy flies for trout grew more and more popular under this prevailing attitude, and the size and materials in the bass version developed rather naturally into what would become known as bass bugs.

The practice of using the gaudy, colorful, and oversized flies for trout, by the way, continued into the 1900s. Many fancy patterns turned into streamers, which were emerging as a separate, distinct class of flies. The rest of the patterns took to the shelves of history with the impact of Theodore Gordon and the rise of the school that sought a more realistic imitation.

The bass bug proper came about as a couple of different traditions converged.

As early as the 1760s, William Bartram reported a technique used by native Americans in the Southeast to capture large-mouth bass. The lure was called a bob, a fist-sized wad of deer hair and feathers wrapped around three hooks bound by their shanks. The bob was suspended from a long pole and worked over the surface of the water from the front of a canoe, as the canoe was worked quietly along the shoreline by a paddler in the stern.[68]

According to McClane, the original cork-bodied bass bugs developed in Missouri and Arkansas, on the Saint Francis and Little rivers. These waters gave rise to local lures stuck together from beer-bottle corks and turkey feathers, well before 1900.[69]

The development of the hair-bug, the spun deer-hair style body, is a mystery. Schullery says Henshall is often acknowledged as creator of the trimmed-hair bass bug, but he fails to give a date for this.

William Bayard Sturgis claims the hair-spinning technique came to Chicago about 1912, brought by Emerson Hough, who found a fly tied in this way on a fishing trip in the "far North." Originally, Sturgis reports, the body was spun with bucktail. Hough and Fred Peet worked with the tying technique through that winter, developing a fly named after Hough. Later, according to Sturgis, tyers switched to deer body hair for spinning.[70]

According to Charles Waterman, it was 1910 or 1911 when Ernest H. Peckinpaugh of Chattanooga, Tennessee, created the first bass bug. He'd made some smaller ones, for panfish, and he enlarged them to appeal to bass. Over the next 20 years bass bugs became big business. Dozens of patterns were produced commercially by the thousands.

In 1934, Peckinpaugh produced the first popping bug, or popper, adding a new dimension to the fly-rod lures, as poppers have a pretty hard time passing for flies, even under an expanded definition of the term.

Bass bugs, like streamers, stretched the definition of fly fishing. There are always curmudgeons who resist adaptation and change, and this expanded role of fly tackle was no exception, but it's pretty much a scream against the wind. There's scarcely an angler around who doesn't acknowledge the growth and expansion that have come to the sport through an expanded definition that has literally moved beyond fly fishing as such into the realm of fly-rod fishing.

Other than the development of a full line of bass bugs and poppers, fly fishing for bass created little in the way of innovative tackle. One possible exception is the bug-taper fly line, a taper configured with a heavy forward portion designed to turn over big, heavy, wind-resistant flies.

The most recent proponent of bass fishing with a fly has been Dave Whitlock, fly tyer extraordinaire. In addition to developing a variety of effective fly patterns for bass, Whitlock has approached bass fishing as a sport that is worthy in and of itself, rather than as a spinoff of trout fishing. This approach has merit, and saltwater fly fishing can also be viewed in the same light.

Every now and then bass fishing is rediscovered. At one point not long ago it was offered up as an alternative to trout fishing in light of the increasingly crowded conditions on trout streams. This was a brilliant bit of marketing perhaps, but without a whole lot of appeal. After all, bass are bass and trout are trout. Even though the same tackle works on each, they are different kinds of fishing, each with its special attributes and attractions. One species scarcely substitutes for the other.

Just about anything that swims is fair game to the fly fisherman. Frontiers are opening up all the time. At one time, in the middle of this century, it was thought Pacific salmon wouldn't take a fly. They would, but the fishery was short-lived. Now they are all but gone, victims of development, pollution, and greed.

Peacock bass, or pavón, are drawing more and more anglers to South America. There is potential too for fly fishing payara and any number of species in the Amazon drainage. Farther south, the frontiers of fly fishing for dorado, a fish little known in North America, hold spectacular promise.

OVERLEAF: *Bonbright Streamer, a tarpon pattern originated circa 1920 by George Bonbright, president of the Seaboard Airline Railway.*

CHAPTER TEN

TOOLS OF THE TRADE

As Skues pointed out so succinctly, the only thing that really changes in fly fishing is the "advance of mechanical conveniences and entomological science."

Of course, mechanical conveniences means our tackle, and the changes made to answer the demands of angling theory, which requires that tackle do certain things, and technology, which gives us materials that behave more efficiently.

Since World War II, when the age of synthetics came along and changed everything, fishing tackle seems to have driven the development of the sport, rather than the other way around, which was the way it had been for centuries. The Age of Spinning — recognized by many as the Dark Ages of Fly Fishing — is a textbook example of this, product driving the sport. With the development of monofilament nylon and spinning reels, fishing — and very effective fishing — was suddenly at everyone's fingertips. There's no way to underestimate the effect these changes had on fishing and fisheries around the world.

In fact, in *American Fly Fishing,* Paul Schullery reports an interview done with Edward Hewitt just before his death. "I hate this whole spinning business," said Hewitt. "It will absolutely ruin all fishing in trout streams. I'd outlaw it if I could. They're using lures and spinners, and they can reach out farther and catch the big ones. And the spawn of a big trout is worth five times as much as the spawn of small ones."

Gradually, over time, the market has come to drive the sport. With the huge growth in fly-fishing participation over the last 20 years, this has been the way many anglers have grown up in the sport. At this point it's neither good nor bad, just different than it was.

We're not going to look at the tackle that is available to anglers today. Like recent fishing history, recent tackle history too easily and too soon becomes boosterism. Tackle shops and magazines do a great job of monitoring what's available. We'll be looking at what has come and gone, and in some cases, come and stayed.

A lot of developments and inventions never take off. Look at boron, which looked like the next big step forward in rodbuilding in the early 80s. It never really caught on, but graphite has gotten stronger and lighter, and captured the rod market. But who knows, in a year or two boron may be the hottest thing going again and may well be the premier rod material for the next 50 years. At that point someone can come along and write how graphite didn't last too long, a brief interlude between glass and boron. There's more tackle available today than most of us can ever fish. Time will sort it out.

RODS: EXERCISING LEVERAGE

Hazel, crab tree, juniper, willow, aspen, blackthorn, yew — these were the materials of fly rods for hundreds of years. Rods were long, lines of equal length; and all casting was done with the wind, allowing the line to float out over the stream and carry the fly with it.

Every period had its favored rod materials. Most were simply discoveries of better materials, rather than innovation that would perform new feats. New feats were few and far between, and modern casting didn't appear until the demands of long casts in West Coast steelheading and modern dry-fly fishing eclipsed the preferred soft-action rod of wet-fly fishing.

A quick rundown reads like this: Chinese anglers used bamboo and thornwood for thousands of years. Dame Juliana recommended a butt of hazel, willow, or aspen, and tip of blackthorn, crab tree, medlar, or juniper. Charles Cotton preferred a fir butt, with a thornwood, juniper, or yew tip.

As soon as American woods were available, English rod makers adopted them. Hickory, for example, found a place in rod-building as soon as it was available. According to John Waller Hills, hickory, lancewood, bamboo, and greenheart became the predominant rod materials, and beginning in the early 1800s, completely replaced hazel, juniper, and a long list of other exotic woods. Hills found hickory mentioned as early as 1760, and again in 1801.

But exporting the wood to Britain, then importing the finished rods again was not an efficient way to do business. It went against the American grain. Just before the Americans took their tackle making into their own hands, a British rod was produced that landed in the American Museum of Fly Fishing 139 years after it was built in 1832. Paul Schullery's description of the rod provides a good look at the conventions of the time.

The rod is 12 feet long, built of five pieces, probably hickory or ash. Fittings are nickel silver, known as German silver. The reel seat sat a foot up from the butt and was the two-ring variety. Ferrules were just sleeves, with a tapered dowel in the center. Guides were the loose-ring type, popular in the mid-nineteenth century.

This rod likely represents the state of the art at the time. It wasn't a casting rod; with a horsehair or a horsehair-and-silk line, its length was the secret to effective line manipulation.

The Americans soon applied themselves to rod-building using the British equipment like this rod for models, developing rods suited to American waters and their relatively unrefined style of angling.

Thaddeus Norris was an early rod designer as well as a writer. He preferred a rod with a white ash butt, a middle section of ironwood, and a four-strip bamboo tip. Norris went into rod-building and became an innovator in the business.

The pre and post-Civil War anglers were different fly fishers. Prior to the Civil War, the angler was a generalist, his tackle adaptable to a variety of fishing styles.[71] He might use the same tackle to fish flies or troll a minnow. Casting was not yet developed enough to require a specialized rod to accomplish it. Stewart, after all, had just begun looking upstream, and the dry fly, by the most conservative estimates, was not yet even recognized as a separate method pattern, and these two developments were what would eventually demand a rod that could be called on to cast a line in any direction. This demand would be met by an American development, the six-strip split-cane rod.

The final triumph of split-cane rod manufacturing was a slow process, and it had a few claimants to its invention. Traditionally, the nod goes to Samuel Phillipe, a gunmaker from Easton, Pennsylvania. Phillipe worked in three and four-strip construction during the 1840s but finally settled on six as the magic number. Dr. James Henshall, whose name appears throughout the history of American fly fishing, verified the fact that Phillipe indeed was the first to develop a workable six-strip split-cane rod and the first to build a trout rod entirely of split cane.

The popularization of the technique came through another true American original, Hiram Leonard.

Skilled hunter, angler, guide, and woodsman, Leonard made a rod in 1871, as a hobbyist. By 1874 he was working in six-strip split cane. Leonard had built a company and sold controlling interest to the Mills Company of New York. In

1881 the company moved to the Hudson Valley, a few miles from New York City.

Leonard is generally credited with popularizing the six-strip rod. His technical innovations as well were substantial. He patented a waterproof ferrule in 1875 and 1878, a critical component when bamboo strips were joined with water-soluble animal glues.

He was one of the first to maintain the hexagonal shape of the six-strip rod, rather than rounding off the corners. Leonard recognized that the essential power fibers lay in the outside layers of the cane, and rounding the rods, which was common previously, deprived the finished product of all the strength and resilience inherent in the bamboo.

Though Leonard is generally recognized as the father of the split-cane rod, his greatest contribution lay in his manufacturing and marketing savvy.

Leonard assembled an impressive lineup of talent in his shop, builders who would eventually break out on their own to produce highly desirable rods for their own merits. Payne, Thomas, Hawes, Philbrook, and Edwards all became innovators in split-cane construction, and all passed through the Leonard shop.

What Leonard's shop did was to apply the principles of industrial manufacturing to fly-rod production. They produced ferrules from tubing rather than from flat stock; they created machines that streamlined the production of fine fly rods, and in doing so they produced rods in the hundreds, instead of in ones and twos, setting the standard and creating the model high-quality, production rod shops to follow.

Charles Orvis began making bamboo rods in the late 1870s. Thomas Chubb put out an enormous number of rods, rods that were far more affordable than those made by Leonard. Sears, Roebuck and Montgomery Ward both put out thousands of affordable and very fishable fly rods.

By the turn of the century, if you fly fished you did it with a split-cane rod, probably nine feet long. Snake guides had become common, and in terms of quality of hardware, craftsmanship, and fittings, you could take your pick. There were plenty available.

Tonkin cane appeared in New York in 1895, and it quickly took over where Calcutta cane had previously been the standard material.

Tonkin cane grows in Guangxi Zhuangzu and Guangdong in southern China, where often fierce tropical monsoon conditions have bred an extremely strong and resilient cane — far more so than other species. This is what makes it so appropriate for rod construction, where compression and elongation of fibers are the name of the game. The fibers in Tonkin cane are efficient at compressing and stretching. It was and is unsurpassed in wood rod making.

Forty years later, the flow of Tonkin cane into the U.S. was severely restricted, then stopped with the attack on Pearl Harbor. Following World War II, an embargo on trade with China and the development of fiberglass as a rod-building material put an end to the mass production of split-cane rods.

Split cane is still available, but it's a high-end market, not much cheaper used than new, a definite collector's market.

Cane has qualities that no other material has, and most of them run to the poetic and highly personal. The fine cane rod is a piece of art, much like a fine musical instrument. It's a world unto itself, and if you care to get into it, there are plenty of materials to guide you on your way. Like Walton, many good anglers become enthralled with split-bamboo rods and devote themselves to their collection and fishing.

Every maker has his trademark construction techniques. Eastern and western rod builders differed in what they felt was important. Light weight was always critical, and the eastern school strove for lighter and lighter rods, often shorter and shorter. Western fishing took place on bigger rivers, and consequently, power was at a premium on these streams. In a quest for more power without more weight, Lew Stoner developed the fluted hollow construction, maintaining plenty of glue surface between segments but eliminating the pithy, nonfunctional core of the cane segments. In 1938, these products of the R.L. Winston Rod Company in San Francisco broke records, with casts of more than 160 feet by G.L. McLeod and Marvin Hedge. Dick Miller cast one of these rods 183 feet, 3 inches the following year.[72]

Rods are collected by name of the builder — Stoner, Powell, Payne, Young, and Garrison.

Bear in mind that if you choose to get in to split-cane rods, you'll have to be thinking in terms of rich glow of the cane itself, the patina of well-worn fittings; even the cases of these rods inspire descriptions usually reserved for wine or music. Move slowly so you don't miss the sturdy richness of saddle leather stitched with waxed linen, or the gleam of old brass catches, the musty odor of poplin and the perfume of tung-oil varnish. Fittings are not just fittings — they are as delicate and lovely as fine old jewelry.

Cane rods also will catch fish, if that's of interest to you. So will fiberglass and graphite.

The first fiberglass rod was built by Dr. Arthur Howald in 1944. By 1946, the Shakespeare Company had gotten hold of the technology and introduced a line of glass fishing rods. The first rods were wood-cored, but this soon fell by the wayside, and Conolon introduced the first hollow fiberglass fly rod, now the most common type of fly rod.

Originally glass rods were expensive — on a par with Leonard's products — but rapidly the price came down. The first glass rods were a far cry from the rods that fly fishermen are able to purchase today, but they rapidly improved and the price came down just as quickly.

In 1978 it was estimated that of the three million rods sold every year in the U.S., not two percent were bamboo.[73] That's a complete takeover of the market.

Metal ferrules had disappeared from the top-of-the-line rods by the mid 60s, replaced by ferrules of fiberglass that nearly eliminated the dead spot created by metal ferrules.

For all its revolutionary qualities, the heyday of fiberglass was far shorter than that of bamboo. By the early 1970s, graphite was on the scene. The first graphite rods had as many problems but they were quickly solved. While graphite rods didn't become as affordable as fiberglass, they still captured the fly-rod market. Boron appeared briefly in the late 70s and 80s but really hasn't gotten much play. Who knows what the next few decades will bring in the way of rod materials.

We're not done yet — and will not be until the perfect rod is developed, a rod that weighs nothing at all and can cast as much line as you are willing to pack on a reel, one that handles the biggest fish quickly and easily and yet has the forgiveness to cushion the finest tippet.

REELS

Reels are a place to store line.

At a recent tackle show I talked to a manufacturer about a beautiful reel he produces — in titanium. The price was laughable. And he laughed. After explaining how the reel functioned as a self-cooling fan while the spool was spinning, he remarked that if you had the reel in your hand and did a re-entry from earth's orbit, you wouldn't survive the experience but the reel would be ready to fish as soon as it hit the ground.

How often do you need that?

A good angler sets a reel on a light setting that won't allow the line to overrun and creates the pressure he needs with his hands. And he can catch most things that swim. The most you ever need is a reel that won't fail, one that won't impede you when you fight heavy fish. Beyond that, premium reels are mostly status symbols of conspicuous consumption.

The Chinese enjoyed the convenience of fishing reels long before the idea ever occurred to the Europeans. Illustrations that came to light in the early 1970s, with the publication of *The History of Chinese Science* by Joseph Needham, clearly show a reel mounted on a fishing rod in a painting called *Angler on a Wintry Lake* by Ma Yuan, and it is easily traced to the Song dynasty in the middle of the twelfth century. The Chinese had a well-developed industry in weaving and spinning, and the concept of the bobbin and winder was well known. It is Schwiebert's conjecture that this technology was readily applied to fishing reels.[74]

In Europe, the reel didn't appear for a while.

In 1651, *The Art of Angling,* the last book published after Berners and before Walton, Thomas Barker mentions a fishing reel, the first time in English. Walton mentioned the reel in 1655, as an accessory to salmon fishing, and a reel appears in Venables' frontispiece, according to John Waller Hills. Also according to Hills, salmon fishermen were employing reels in the early 1700s and trout anglers used them from 1750 on, but these reels were "plain barrel winders of brass." Hills cites an advertisement in 1770. Mentioned again, in Best's *Concise Treatise on the Art of Angling* in 1787, Hills concludes it must not have been uncommon practice to use a reel to hold line.

Reels were where Americans really took off in innovation. The famed and well-recognized Kentucky watch makers produced the first completely American tackle. These reels were multipliers (a reel design in which one turn of the handle produces more than one revolution in the spool), the watch maker's trade created in a winding device, and like the rods, they weren't especially limited to fly fishing.

The first single-action reel patented was in 1859, by William Billinghurst, but his reel bore little resemblance to the reels that would follow in the first great surge of tackle manufacturing that followed the Civil War.

The Conroy reels, which appeared about 1873, and Vom Hofe's, distinctive with black rubber side plates, share an intertwined history. Basically, though the machining was exquisite and the workmanship topnotch, these were single-action fly reels, good storage units for line. Their history is perhaps interesting in itself, but they had little to do with the way fishing was conducted.

In 1874, Orvis obtained a patent on its reel, a perforated pattern designed to dry the line and reduce weight. The standard for American fly reels was established with this design.

Everything else was virtually a repeat of the theme. The only real advance in fly reel design has been in drags, and these reels have been designed for salmon and saltwater fish, with an emphasis on the latter. Saltwater fly fishing requires strong, smooth, and reliable drags. A lot of this technology was borrowed from offshore reels, and synthetic materials for drag discs have opened a new world of technical innovation.

One last work — the automatic reel — appeared in the late 1800s. The automatic never seems to have had any real champions or adherents, but somehow it is still with us. Somebody must be using them, because they are still available.

LINES: THE ESSENTIAL LINK

The original fishing lines were lengths of horsehair spliced together. Juliana Berners recommended dyeing horsehair different colors for different seasons of the year; Cotton prescribed a tapered line, as related earlier, from the white hairs of a horse's tail. By decreasing the number of hairs used, section by section, a tapered line was created with the least thickness of hairs ending in the attachment of the fly.

Silk was the second material to be used for fly-line construction — though the term "fly line," specialized as it is today, was hardly the product then that it is now, with its description of weight and taper to denote form and function.

Hair and silk were combined for a long time, though the uneven stretch and resistance of the two materials created constant problems.

Silk lines first appeared in the literature in Nobbes' *Compleat Troller* in 1682, but hair lines stuck around well through, and Hills recalls hair lines used by old-timers through the end of the 1800s as well, and adds (writing in 1921), no doubt "some could be found even now."

Enamel-finished line became common near the end of the nineteenth century. Level lines made of raw braided silk and oil-impregnated appeared around 1875.

Eaton & Deller, a British firm, produced the first true forerunner to our modern tapered lines, a woven, tapered silk line, oil-dressed.

Frederick Halford became heavily involved with the design of fly lines, working towards a woven, fast-taper design, impregnated with oil and polished to a gloss finish. These Halford designs were the standard of quality for the first half of the twentieth century. These lines required drying after every use, and they absorbed water.

Braided silk lines were considerably heavier for their diameter than modern nylon lines. This means the lines of a given weight were far thinner, and thus handled differently. These lines were the state of the art until after World War II, when braided nylon lines became available.

Double taper was the prime configuration, and it took the innovative ideas born of the casting clubs on the California coast to move beyond these to the weight-forward taper and shooting-tapers that allowed the additional distance necessary to fish the brawny western rivers.

One of the biggest problems with nylon-coated lines was their elasticity. Not until the development of polyvinyl chloride (PVC) coatings was this problem solved. This took place about 1949, and a few years later the taper problem was solved when techniques were discovered for tapering the coating over a level braided core. The modern fly line had been born.

Tapered silk lines had been designated by diameters. Diameters were tagged with letters of the alphabet, from A, which was .060 inches, to I, which was .022 inches. A popular taper would have been HDH and HCH; heavier work would have required a GBG, and a skilled hand with a very light rod might have opted for an HEH.

With the development of nylon cores, these diameters stayed the same but the weight of the lines changed because nylon was much lighter than silk in a given diameter.

Again, the West Coast anglers were well ahead of the game. All the while they had been developing specialized tapers, derived from the demands of steelhead and salmon fishing, but adapted to the demands of the tournament pond. Their understanding of fly-line tapers, weights, and diameters was second to none. With the advent of Dacron and nylon cores and polyvinyl chloride coatings, Myron Gregory developed a line classification system based on the weight in grains of the first 30 feet of fly line. Gregory codified the sizes, and Art Agnew of Sunset Line and Twine in Petaluma, California, took on the job of selling the new designations to the tackle industry. The job they set about to do stuck. This is the same system we have today.

The final portion of the line, the leader, changed drastically twice in history. Early in the eighteenth century, silkworm gut began to move into popular usage, and by the time the Civil War rolled around, it was the standard.

Gut was of notoriously inconsistent quality. It was never strong enough to handle the very biggest fish, nor fine enough to fish very tiny flies. Still, there were plenty of anglers who fished their entire careers with gut leaders.

The final switchover in leader material came just after World War II, when nylon leader material became available for fly fishermen. Stiff, with plenty of memory, the first nylons were difficult to work with, but soon the technology improved, and today nylons are available in sizes and strengths that were unthinkable in the days of gut.

PUTTING THE TWO TOGETHER

The single distinguishing characteristic of fly fishing, the thing that sets it apart most from other types of fishing, is the casting. This distinctive modern casting is something that grew up with the development of lines and rods.

As we've learned, until the upstream dry-fly technique became the fishing standard, all casting was a slow development from the wind-driven cast. The spey and roll casts developed in salmon fishing, but these lacked the essential motion of modern casting.

The first published casting instructions called for the rod tip to be swept in an elongated circle, so the line didn't travel in the same plane on the back cast as the forecast. This approach remained popular into the late 1800s. Henshall advocated this type of casting. As well, in spite of the developments to come, Henshall proclaimed that a caster was proficient enough to call himself a fisherman when he could hit his hat eight times out of 10 at 40 feet. There are still writers who maintain that same criterion.

It was the development of silk lines and split-cane rods that opened the door for modern precision casting techniques. In tournaments during the 1880s, casts of 80 feet were common, and salmon-rod competitors were reaching over 100 feet.

No matter how well equipment functioned, or how many fish were caught, the yearning for greater distance is part and parcel of fly casting. Maybe it is so with any fishing, but other forms of casting don't involve the same level of athletic accomplishment and training as fly casting.

Once silk lines and rigid snake guides were standard issue, line could be manipulated with the left hand sufficiently to speed up the cast and increase distance, and the double haul was a natural development.

Some historians speculate the double haul was a pretty closely kept secret. The distance tournaments where the haul would have been best developed were very competitive, with individuals' and companies' reputations on the line.

Tournament records indicate a substantial jump in distance casts in 1897 when a caster from San Francisco jumped the winning cast by about 20 feet. The Californians seemed to have an edge, winning with substantially longer casts than was the norm for the Easterners.

Throughout the first couple decades of the twentieth century, there were hints in the literature of double-haul technique. Then in 1934, Marvin Hedge formally presented the double haul at a tournament in St. Louis. He went on to global prominence, outcasting European champion Albert Godart, and broke the British record as well.

The double haul had come of age in casting. It varied, caster to caster, from the powerful, effective long pull perfected by Hedge, that McClane called the "underwear ripping motion," to a short, precisely placed tug that worked just as well.

The most significant landmark in modern casting theory came with the publication of *Fly Casting with Lefty Kreh* in 1974. Basing his theory on modern tackle, Lefty completely dismantled the jumbled collection of casting precepts that had accumulated over the previous hundred years, sorted them out, discarded the useless, and developed the techniques best suited to fishing. It was a landmark publication. Though most anglers just looked at the pictures, those few who read the text and studied what Lefty was getting at found their casting transformed. Over the past decades, Lefty has transformed American casting, applying principles based on modern tackle to take full advantage of what is possible.

REPLICAS OF FISH FOOD

In the study of artificial flies lies the true history of fly fishing. A knowledgeable angler, given a fly from any period, would likely end up fishing that fly in the way it was designed to be fished. There's a world of study in the history of fly tying — fly dressing, as the British tradition dictates — and there's far more to study than we have space for here. This, then, is a brief outline.

Juliana Berners described the first set of flies, "the XII," in *TFA,* and until Bowlker cleaned house, these patterns were pirated and reworked by any number of writers. The publication of Bowlker's *Art of Angling* in 1747 marked the beginning of modern fly dressing.[75]

Bowlker assembled a new list, which was promptly classicized, as John McDonald describes it, for the second half of the eighteenth century.

The wet fly had been fully developed and was a mature form of fly 25 years before Ronalds' *Fly-Fisher's Entomology* came out in 1836.[76]

While the tradition of fly dressing progressed in Great Britain, it didn't develop in the same way in America — in fact, once again it is necessary to look at the two continents separately, as well as at how they influenced each other.

The sparse dressing of the English, "the XII," dominated fly dressing for two centuries. Cotton next described variations, comparing his own delicate Derbyshire flies with the laughable stout and, to his eye, ill-proportioned flies of the chalkstreams south of London.

At this time, most of the major salmonid fisheries in Great Britain had their own style of fly dressing.

Alfred Ronalds, as discussed earlier, took an important step when he linked artificials to a specific natural insect. Fly dressing took on a precision of imitation it hadn't known before.

Standard wet-fly patterns still varied regionally, and many of the wet flies looked like dry flies. There had to have been a large period of gray area, when wet flies were fished floating, but dry-fly technique had not yet been established. Wet flies were certainly fished in the surface film, and the winging and hackling styles of what were considered wet flies needed little except a shake-off on the false cast to sit on the surface film and become dry flies.

George Pulman described the first dry flies in *The Vade Mecum of Fly-Fishing for Trout* published in 1840.

From 1850 onward, the spread of the dry fly throughout England and Scotland was steady and thorough.

Caddis imitations, long the backbone of wet-fly fishing, also began to be fished floating, and by 1900 dry caddis imitations had been developed in England.

Extended-body flies, mayfly imitations, also were developed before 1900. Halford sported several of these in his kit.

Spinner imitations, spent-wing patterns, were also worked out in the late nineteenth century, credited to William Lunn, riverkeeper of the Houghton Club on the Test.

The British wet-fly patterns and the salmon patterns were the first to be used in the New World. Where the Americans really took off and developed their own patterns was in the development of the "fancy flies" of the late 1800s.

These were spin-offs from the salmon flies of England for the most part. Most of them were strictly attractor patterns, or so we consider them today in retrospect. Bright colors, gaudy combinations, and ostentatious assembly typified the fancy flies. Brook trout were hardly the discerning and selective fish of the English chalkstreams. Bass as well, common sight-feeders, tended towards the ample in fly preference, so these colorful, heavily dressed patterns served well.

Schullery has said it best when he explains, "The American fancy fly was . . . a folk art response to a variety of fishes whose feeding habits did not constrain the fly fisher to worry overly much about accurate imitation of fish food types."[77]

Some writers have given a lot of ink to the theory that the fancy flies were an American response to independence from the British, a celebration of anarchy in fly design. Sounds like the topic for a master's thesis. Basically, Americans tied and fished the fancy flies for the same reasons you and I would if we could: because they were fun and they worked.

The world of Victorian trade supplied exotic and soon-to-be rare animal furs and feathers in an unprecedented abundance, and one that would never be possible again. Fish took the flies readily, and until they became more selective, tyers' imaginations were free to run wild in designing fishing flies. Who would settle for woodcock or rolled duck flanks when red and white married swan wings worked just as well?

The age of the fancy fly found its most complete expression in Mary Orvis Marbury's *Favorite Flies and Their Histories*, a catalogue of nearly 300 fly patterns illustrated in color.

Marbury was the daughter of Charles Orvis, founder of the tackle company that is still with us today. She was in charge of the company's fly-tying and was in a singular position to publish the definitive catalogue of patterns in 1892.

By the end of the nineteenth century, the rolled-wing style of dry fly came into prominence in the Catskill school of fly tying. Gordon originated it and passed it on to Roy Steenrod and Reuben Cross. Harry and Elsie Darbee were the most recent carriers of the torch. Catskill style was typified by sparsely tied, delicate flies, an economy of thread and materials suggesting at once a general and specific imitation. The Gordon Quill and Hendrickson are both archetypes.

Hair wings developed on Big Spring Creek in Idaho in 1901, when a Chicago angler tied up the first swept-wing fly as a farce, using dog hair, while a guest on the Trude ranch. The Trude has since carved a historical niche for itself as a general caddis and stonefly imitator.

Caddis imitation got a big boost in 1972 with the publication of *Fishing the Dry Fly as a Living Insect* by Leonard Wright. Subsequent writers have given the caddisfly about as much treatment as it can stand, though the benefit of this has been that caddis imitations — adults and emergers — finally have the recognition they deserve, and anglers are catching a lot more fish because of it.

The Wulff series has carved an even better-known niche. Lee Wulff designed the hair-wing mayfly imitations, the story goes, and Dan Bailey had them tied up in his Livingston, Montana, shop, fishing them, promoting them, and selling them. Although developed for eastern fishing, they remain a classic western pattern, part attractor, part imitator. There are shops all over Montana where about the first of August if you drop in and ask if the fish are hitting Royal Wulffs yet, the answer is apt to be, "No, but they are starting to howl at night."

The first use of hair as a wing material no doubt predated the Wulff patterns, but Wulff made them popular. They will be forever linked with his name.

The Midwest also had its patterns. One of the prevailing patterns in the last half century is a nondescript gray mayfly, tied by Leonard Halladay in 1922. It debuted at the hands of a Chicago lawyer, Charles Adams, after whom it was named.

The woman who gained fame for her tying in New York City and whom Gingrich referred to as the "First Lady of Fly Tying," Helen Shaw, lived in Wisconsin.

Nearby Minnesota was home to George Herter, who entered the tackle-making and fly-tying business in the 1930s and commanded a virtual empire in terms of mail-order sporting goods.

Herter was the first and last of the great self-promoters. His catalogues and his books were filled with unmitigated hype, thoroughly full of fishing and fly-tying lore and thoroughly entertaining to read. Even his catalogues were a tremendous amount of fun. George Herter also made fly fishing available, and kept it available to millions of anglers. He maintained a proletarian approach. That's where the business was, and Herter was above all a businessman.

More recently, the age of synthetics had and is still having a major impact on fly tying. Saltwater flies especially are often made entirely of plastic materials, materials that surpass natural materials in their suitability for flies. Initial attempts at categorizing marine organisms to be imitated are a bit inflated. The saltwater angler still hasn't found a way, a codification, like freshwater anglers have. Maybe he never will. The variety and abundance of saltwater food organisms is vast and may be far too complex to codify. Or maybe we're in the infancy. It's not yet history, so it's too soon to tell.

BOOKS AND PEOPLE

Books and people are also tools and resources in fly fishing. Those who have not yet had the opportunity to stand the test of time still offer a lot to the sport as a living entity.

Many of the anglers who make the sport what it is today are still alive. Many anglers who are still alive would like to feel they have made the sport what it is. It's a tough call, and I'm going to lean heavily on dead men once again.

Ray Bergman, Joe Brooks, and Al McClane are the three anglers everyone would like to have fished with. Thousands of anglers grew up reading these men in the magazines, and they are part of nearly everyone's fishing today.

One of the more controversial figures in the twentieth century has been Lee Wulff. Many idolize him as a generation before idolized Gordon, while others view him as an opportunist and public-relations invention. There's no settling the issue, but it's pretty clear Wulff is going to go down in history for all but inventing modern fly fishing. He is credited with inventing the fishing vest, the exposed rim reel, short fly rods, catch-and-release fishing, and hair-wing dry flies.

Whether or not he invented all these things is beside the point. He popularized them and publicized so many things about fly fishing that he's become one of the true luminaries in the sport.

Arnold Gingrich, founding editor of *Esquire* magazine, is a tremendous part of the literary history of fly fishing. *The Fishing in Print, The Joys of Trout,* and *The Well-Tempered Angler* are indispensable titles to the well-read fly fisherman of today. Gingrich died in 1976, just a few days earlier than his friend Charles Ritz.

Ritz, of the famed European hotel family, was a dedicated fisherman, rod designer, and casting expert. His designs for Pezon & Michel yielded the parabolic action — which Ritz preferred to call the progressive action — nonetheless, it's a part of our kit today. So is *A Fly Fisher's Life,* published in English in 1959. Ritz was a firm believer in training for casting, both in techniques and strength of the casting arm, and he was way ahead of his time.

In 1969, the sport's first periodical was born. Don Zahner launched the magazine *Fly Fisherman* in St. Louis, and the response was tremendous. The first promotional mailing to drum up subscriptions produced a 50-percent return. This is in a game in which four percent response is considered a victory. Evidently, there was a need, and room for competition, too. Ten years later, John Merwin, *Fly Fisherman*'s managing editor, left *Fly Fisherman* and founded *Rod & Reel,* which began as a magazine for all anglers but soon specialized in fly fishing.

Over the past couple of decades, much that has been written about fly fishing has been brought back into print, and Nick Lyons is perhaps the biggest single reason. At Crown, Winchester, and now his own house, Lyons has made a tremendous contribution to the sport by maintaining and reissuing a long list of great books that would now be unavailable were it not for his stubborn dedication to the printed word.

Working writers can be important to fishing, too. Roderick Haig-Brown wrote better than just about anyone about trout, salmon, rivers, fishing, and life from his home in Campbell River in British Columbia.

In our own time, perhaps the most influential person in fly fishing has been author Norman Maclean, or perhaps Robert Redford who produced the movie from Maclean's novella *A River Runs Through It.* That may sound cynical, but it's true. The impact of what has come to be known as The Movie is unprecedented. That's not a value judgment, just an observation. This impact is especially interesting in light of the words of one of the most overlooked observers of all, Richard Brautigan.

Brautigan didn't describe any fly patterns or invent any that I know of. But he saw more clearly the course of American fishing. And he gave us a description and a glimpse into his fishing mind, and our own, that few writers ever attempt.

Just as Izaak Walton came along to describe the lifestyle of the angler, Brautigan came along and presented the landscape of the mind that accompanies all good angling. And he placed our fishing in a modern context. Who's ever the same after reading Brautigan's chapter "The Cleveland Wrecking Yard" where the writer sees a sign that says "Used Trout Stream for Sale"? The salesman explains.

> "We're selling it by the foot length. You can buy as little as you want or you can buy all we've got left. . . . We're selling the waterfalls separately of course, and the trees and birds, flowers, grass and ferns we're also selling extra. The insects we're giving away free with a minimum purchase of ten feet of stream."
>
> "How much are you selling the stream for?" I asked.
>
> "Six dollars and fifty cents a foot," he said. "That's for the first hundred feet. After that it's five dollars a foot."
>
> "How much are the birds?" I asked.
>
> "Thirty-five cents apiece," he said. "But of course they're used. We can't guarantee anything."
>
> Stacked over against the wall were the waterfalls. There were about a dozen of them, ranging from a drop of a few feet to a drop of ten or fifteen feet. The waterfalls had price tags on them. They were more expensive than the stream. The waterfalls were selling for $19.00 a foot.[78]

When it comes to quoting fishing writers, there is no end. Fly fishing especially has a wonderful literature attached to it. When you read about the sport, you come to know its heroes and legends, and when you know them, as much as you might idolize them, you know too that, like you, they are just fishermen.

In 1964 Robert Traver published *Anatomy of a Fisherman,* a collection of essays and photos celebrating his angling in Michigan. Included in the book was this chapter, which has become one of the seminal essays in fly fishing:

Testament of a Fisherman

I fish because I love to; because I love the environs where trout are found, which are invariably beautiful, and hate the environs where crowds of people are found, which are invariably ugly; because of all the television commercials, cocktail parties and assorted social posturing I thus escape; because in a world where most men seem to spend their lives doing things they hate, my fishing is at once an endless source of delight and act of small rebellion; because trout do not lie or cheat and cannot be bought or bribed or impressed by power, but respond only to quietude and humility and endless patience; because I suspect that men are going along this way for the last time and I for one don't want to waste the trip; because mercifully there are no telephones on trout waters; because only in the woods can I find solitude without loneliness; because bourbon out of an old tin cup always tastes better out there; because maybe one day I will catch a mermaid; and, finally, not because I regard fishing as being so terribly important but because I suspect that so many of the other concerns of men are equally unimportant — and not nearly so much fun.

NOTES

ENDNOTES

1. Hans Jorgen Hurum, *A History of the Fish Hook* (London: Adam & Charles Black, 1976), 30.

2. William Radcliffe, *Fishing From Earliest Times* (London: John Murray, 1926), iii.

3. Ernest Schwiebert, *Trout* (New York: Dutton, 1984), 13.

4. Radcliffe, *Fishing From the Earliest Times,* 187-189.

5. John McDonald, *Quill Gordon* (New York: Knopf, 1972), 127.

6. John Waller Hills, *A History of Fly Fishing for Trout* (Rockville Centre, N.Y.: Freshet Press, 1971), 12.

7. A.J. McClane, *Fishing with McClane* (Englewood Cliffs, N.J.: Prentice Hall, 1975), 219.

8. Arnold Gingrich, *The Fishing in Print* (New York: Winchester Press, 1974), 27.

9. Hills, *A History.*

10. A.J. McClane, *McClane's New Standard Fishing Encyclopedia and International Angling Guide* (New York: Holt, 1974), 1073-1074.

11. Hills, *A History.*

12. John Buchan, introduction to *The Compleat Angler* by Izaak Walton and Charles Cotton (Oxford and New York: Oxford University Press, 1982).

13. Hills, *A History,* 65-66.

14. Hills, *A History,* 83.

15. Hills, *A History,* 96.

16. Schwiebert, *Trout,* 83.

17. Hills, *A History,* 69.

18. Hills, *A History,* 94.

19. Hills, *A History,* 75.

20. Hills, *A History,* 77.

21. McClane, *McClane's,* 387.

22. G.E.M. Skues, *Minor Tactics of the Chalk Stream* (London: Adam & Charles Black, 1910), 13.

23. John Waller Hills, *A Summer on the Test* (London, 1930).

24. Skues, *Minor Tactics,* 23.

25. Don Zahner, *Anglish Spoken Here* (Lexington, Mass.: Stephen Green Press, 1986), 36.

26. Art Lee, "Hampshire Chalkstreams," *Gray's Sporting Journal* (v. 3, issue 3, 1978): 20.

27. Paul Schullery, *American Fly Fishing: A History* (New York: Nick Lyons Books, 1987), 14.

28. Schullery, *American Fly Fishing,* 23.

29. Gingrich, *The Fishing in Print.*

30. McClane, *McClane's,* 453.

31. McClane, *McClane's,* 455.

32. McClane, *McClane's,* 453.

33. Frank Forester, appendix to *The Complete Angler* (New York: Wiley, 1852), 149.

34. Gingrich, *The Fishing in Print,* 151.

35. Schullery, *American Fly Fishing,* 49.

36. Schullery, *American Fly Fishing,* 55-57.

37. Schullery, *American Fly Fishing,* 115.

38. John McDonald, in *The Compleat Fly Fisherman: The Notes and Letters of Theodore Gordon* (New York: Lyons & Burford, 1989), lvii.

39. McDonald, in *The Complete Fly Fisherman*, lvi.

40. McClane, *McClane's*, 526.

41. Frederic M. Halford, *The Dry-Fly Man's Handbook* (New York: Dutton; London: Routledge, 1913), 72.

42. McClane, *McClane's*, 109.

43. Schwiebert, *Trout*, 172.

44. Schwiebert, introduction to *The Art of Tying the Wet Fly and Fishing the Flymph* by James Leisenring and Vernon S. Hidy (New York: Crown, 1971), 19.

45. Trey Combs, *Steelhead Fly Fishing and Flies*, 36.

46. Rex Gerlach, *Fly Fishing for Rainbows* (Harrisburg, Pa.: Stackpole Books, 1988), 19-21.

47. John Merwin, *The New American Trout Fishing* (New York: Macmillan), 9.

48. Cecil Heacox, *The Complete Brown Trout* (New York: Winchester Press, 1974), 14-20.

49. John Monnett, *Cutthroat and Campfire Tales: The Fly Fishing Heritage of the West*, quoted from *Fly Fishing the South Platte River* by Roger Hill (Boulder, Colo.: Pruett Publishing, 1991), xvi.

50. George W. Wingate, *Through the Yellowstone Park on Horseback* (New York: Judd, 1886), 181.

51. Charles E. Brooks, *The Living River* (Garden City, N.Y.: Doubleday, 1979), 56.

52. Paul Schullery, *American Fly Fishing*, 187.

53. George Grant, *The Master Fly Weaver* (Portland, Ore.: Champoeg Press, 1980), 33.

54. Bud Lilly and Paul Schullery, *A Trout's Best Friend: The Angling Autobiography of Bud Lilly* (Boulder, Colo.: Pruett Publishing, 1988), 43.

55. Bud Lilly and Paul Schullery, *Bud Lilly's Guide to Western Fly Fishing* (New York: Nick Lyons Books, 1987), 149.

56. Schullery, *American Fly Fishing*, 157.

57. A.W. Dimock and Julian A. Dimock, *Florida Enchantments* (New York: Outing Publishing Co., 1908).

58. Paul Schullery, *Saltwater Fly Fishing*, 154.

59. J. Edson Leonard, *Flies* (New York: Nick Lyons Books, 1988), 315.

60. Capt. Bill Smith, speaking to C.P. Heaton, "First Bonefish on a Fly," *Florida Sportsman Magazine* (Feb. 1990).

61. George X. Sand, *Salt Water Fly Fishing* (New York: Knopf, 1970), 8-18.

62. Vic Dunaway, "The First Ever, Flying for Tarpon," *Florida Sportsman Magazine* (Apr. 1993).

63. Vic Dunaway, *Modern Saltwater Fishing* (New York: Winchester Press, 1975), 251-262.

64. Trey Combs, *Steelhead Fly Fishing and Flies*, 39.

65. Charles F. Waterman, *Modern Fresh & Salt Water Fly Fishing* (New York: Winchester Press, 1972), 81.

66. Schullery, *American Fly Fishing*, 146.

67. Dave Whitlock, *L.L. Bean Fly Fishing for Bass Handbook* (New York: Nick Lyons Books, 1988), ix.

68. Schullery, *American Fly Fishing*, 20.

69. A.J. McClane, *The Practical Fly Fisherman* (New York: Lyons & Burford, 1989), 109.

70. William Bayard Sturgis, *Fly Tying* (New York: Scribner's, 1940), 197.

71. Schullery, *American Fly Fishing*, 40.

72. McClane, *The Practical Fly Fisherman*, 17.

73. Schwiebert, *Trout*, 1098.

74. Schwiebert, *Trout*, 13.

75. Hills, *A History*, 88-89.

76. Schwiebert, *Trout*, 707.

77. Schullery, *American Fly Fishing*, 78-79.

78. Richard Brautigan, *Trout Fishing in America* (New York: Dell, 1967), 104-106.

BIBLIOGRAPHY

Babson, Stanley. *Bonefishing*. New York: Winchester Press, 1973.

Bergman, Ray. *Trout*. 3d ed. New York: Knopf, 1976.

Brautigan, Richard. *Trout Fishing in America*. New York: Dell, 1967.

Brooks, Charles E. *The Living River*. Garden City, N.Y.: Nick Lyons Books; Doubleday, 1979.

——— *The Trout and the Stream*. Piscataway, N.J.: Nick Lyons Books; Winchester Press, 1974.

Brooks, Joe. *Trout Fishing*. New York: Harper and Row, 1972.

Calabi, Silvio. *The Illustrated Encyclopedia of Fly Fishing*. New York: Holt, 1993.

Chatham, Russell. *The Angler's Coast*. Livingston, Mont.: Clark City Press, 1990.

Combs, Trey. *Steelhead Fly Fishing*. New York: Lyons & Burford, 1991.

Darbee, Harry, and Francis, Mac. *Catskill Flytier: My Life, Times and Techniques*. Philadelphia: Lippincott, 1977.

Dennys, John. *The Secrets of Angling*. 1613. Rockville Centre: Freshet Press, 1970.

Dimock, A.W. *Book of the Tarpon*. 1911. Stone Harbor, N.J.: Meadow Run Press, 1990.

Dimock, A.W., and Julian A. *Florida Enchantments*. New York: Outing Publishing Co., 1908.

Dunaway, Vic. *Modern Saltwater Fishing*. New York: Winchester Press, 1975.

Flick, Art. *Art Flick's New Streamside Guide to Naturals and Their Imitations*. New York: Crown, 1969.

Fox, Charles. *This Wonderful World of Trout*. Rev. ed. Rockville Centre, N.Y.: Freshet Press, 1971.

Francis, Francis. *Angling Reminiscences*. London: Horace Cox, 1887.

Gingrich, Arnold. *The Fishing in Print: A Guided Tour Through Five Centuries of Angling Literature*. New York: Winchester Press, 1974.

Gordon, Theodore. *The Complete Fly Fisherman: The Notes and Letters of Theodore Gordon*. Edited by John McDonald. 1947. New York: Lyons & Burford, 1989.

Grant, George. *The Master Fly Weaver*. Portland, Ore.: Champoeg Press, 1980.

Halford, Frederic M. *The Dry-Fly Man's Handbook: A Complete Manual Including the Fisherman's Entomology and the Making and Management of a Fishery*. New York: Dutton; London: Routledge, 1913.

Heacox, Cecil E. *The Compleat Brown Trout*. New York: Winchester Press, 1974.

Henkin, Harmon. *The Complete Fisherman's Catalog*. Philadelphia: Lippincott, 1977.

Herter, George Leonard. *Professional Fly Tying and Tackle Making Manual and Manufacturer's Guide*. 1941. Waseca, Minn.: Brown Publishing, 1953.

Hill, Roger. *Fly Fishing the South Platte River*. Boulder, Colo.: Pruett Publishing, 1991.

Hills, John Waller. *A History of Fly Fishing for Trout*. 1921. Edited by Richard Eggert. Rockville Centre, N.Y.: Freshet Press, 1971.

Jardine, Charles. *The Classic Guide to Fly-Fishing for Trout*. New York: Random House, 1991.

Jennings, Preston. *A Book of Trout Flies*. New York: Derrydale, 1935.

Kreh, Lefty. *Fly Casting with Lefty Kreh*. Philadelphia: Lippincott, 1974.

——— *Fly Fishing in Salt Water*. 1974. Rev. ed. New York: Nick Lyons Books; Winchester Press, 1986.

——— *Longer Fly Casting*. New York: Lyons & Burford, 1991.

LaBranche, George M.L., *The Dry Fly & Fast Water and The Salmon & the Dry Fly*, Arno Press, New York, 1967.

Leisenring, James, and Hidy, Vernon S. *The Art of Tying the Wet Fly and Fishing the Flymph*. 5th printing. New York: Crown, 1977.

Leonard, J. Edson. *Flies*. New York: Nick Lyons Books, 1988.

Lilly, Bud, and Schullery, Paul. *Bud Lilly's Guide to Western Fly Fishing*. New York: Nick Lyons Books, 1987.

———— *A Trout's Best Friend: The Angling Autobiography of Bud Lilly.* Boulder, Colo.: Pruett Publishing, 1988.

Marinaro, Vincent C. *In the Ring of the Rise.* New York: Crown, 1976.

Marshall, Mel. *Steelhead.* New York: Winchester Press, 1973.

McClane, A.J. *Fishing with McClane.* Edited by George Reiger. Englewood Cliffs, N.J.: Prentice Hall, 1975.

———— *McClane's New Standard Fishing Encyclopedia and International Angling Guide.* Enl. and rev. ed. New York: Holt, 1974.

———— *The Practical Fly Fisherman.* 1953. New York: Lyons & Burford, 1989.

McDonald, John. *Quill Gordon.* New York: Knopf, 1972.

Merwin, John. *The New American Trout Fishing.* New York: Macmillan, 1994.

Norris, Thaddeus. *The American Angler's Book.* Philadelphia: Porter & Coates; London: Sampson Low Son & Co., 1864. Rev. ed.

Orvis, Charles F., and Cheney, A. Nelson. *Fishing with the Fly.* Troy, N.Y.: H.R. Nims, 1885.

Radcliffe, William. *Fishing From the Earliest Times.* 2d ed. London: John Murray, 1926.

Ritz, Charles. *A Fly Fisher's Life.* Translated by Humphrey Hare. London: Max Reinhardt, 1959.

Ronalds, Alfred. *The Fly-Fisher's Entomology.* Facsimile ed. New Jersey: Wellfleet Press, 1990.

Sand, George X. *Salt Water Fly Fishing.* New York: Knopf, 1970.

Schullery, Paul. *American Fly Fishing: A History.* New York: Nick Lyons Books, 1987.

Schwiebert, Ernest. *Matching the Hatch.* New York: Macmillan, 1955.

———— *Trout.* 2d ed. New York: Dutton, 1984.

Scott, Jock. *Greased Line Fishing for Salmon (and Steelhead).* Portland, Ore.: Frank Amato Publications, 1982.

Skues, G.E.M. *The Angling Letters of G.E.M. Skues.* Edited by C.F. Walker. London: Adam & Charles Black, 1956.

———— *Minor Tactics of the Chalk Stream.* London: Adam & Charles Black, 1910.

———— *Nymph Fishing for Chalk Stream Trout.* London: Adam & Charles Black, 1939.

———— *The Way of a Trout with a Fly.* 4th ed. London: Adam & Charles Black, 1949.

Stewart, Dick, and Allen, Farrow. *Flies for Bass & Panfish.* Invale, N.H.: Northland Press, 1992.

Stewart, W.C. *The Practical Angler.* London: Black, 1893.

Sturgis, William Bayard. *Fly-Tying.* New York: Scribner's, 1940.

Swisher, Doug, and Richards, Carl. *Fly Fishing Strategy.* New York: Crown, 1975.

Traver, Robert, and Kelley, Robert W. *Anatomy of a Fisherman.* New York: McGraw Hill, 1964.

Walton, Izaak. *The Complete Angler.* 5th ed. 1676. Edited by Jonquil Bevan. Rutland, Vt.: Everyman, 1993.

Walton, Izaac, and Cotton, Charles. *The Complete Angler.* Edited by G. Bethune. New York: Wiley, 1852.

———— *The Compleat Angler.* 6th ed. 1676. Edited by John Buxton. Oxford and New York: Oxford University Press, 1982.

Waterman, Charles F. *Fly Rodding for Bass.* New York: Nick Lyons Books; Lyons & Burford, 1989.

———— *A History of Angling.* Tulsa, Okla.: Winchester Press, 1981.

———— *Modern Fresh & Salt Water Fly Fishing.* New York: Winchester Press, 1972.

Wells, Henry Parkhurst. *Fly-Rods and Fly-Tackle.* New York: Harper, 1885.

Whitlock, Dave. *L.L. Bean Fly Fishing for Bass Handbook.* New York: Nick Lyons Books, 1988.

Wingate, George W. *Through the Yellowstone Park on Horseback.* New York: Judd, 1886.

Wright, Leonard. *Fishing the Dry Fly as a Living Insect.* 1972. New York: Nick Lyons Books, 1988.

Zahner, Don. *Anglish Spoken Here.* Lexington, Mass.: Stephen Greene Press, 1986.

INDEX